The Ohio Citizen

The Ohio Citizen

ACHIEVING PROFICIENCY IN CITIZENSHIP

J. Mark Stewart
James A. Norris

When ordering this book, please specify:
either **R 590 S** *or* THE OHIO CITIZEN

AMSCO SCHOOL PUBLICATIONS, INC.
315 Hudson Street / New York, N.Y. 10013

Dr. J. Mark Stewart is the Social Studies Supervisor, Columbus Public Schools, Columbus, Ohio. He received a doctorate from Ohio State University and taught social studies for many years.

James A. Norris is the Department Chair, Social Studies, Linden McKinley High School, Columbus, Ohio. A graduate of Ohio State University, he has taught for more than 20 years in Ohio public schools.

ISBN 0-87720-883-2

Printed in the United States of America

10 11 12 13 14   06 05 04 03 02

PREFACE

Ohio's Citizenship Proficiency Test is taken for the first time by 9th-grade students in the state. The test focuses on 17 learning outcomes (see pages vii–viii) and consists of 50 multiple-choice questions. If you do not pass the test in the 9th grade, you may take it again at a later date, but you *must* pass at some time in order to receive a high school diploma.

This book, THE OHIO CITIZEN, was written to help you attain the 17 outcomes in citizenship and thereby do well on the state test. There are 17 chapters in the book, each providing information on a different learning outcome. In addition, there are two practice tests that are similar in design and content to the actual Citizenship Proficiency Test you will be taking.

The Chapters and the Learning Outcomes   To make the best use of a book, you should know how that book is organized. Each chapter of THE OHIO CITIZEN consists of (1) a statement of the learning outcome, (2) a narrative that presents the information to be learned or skills to be mastered, and (3) exercises for reviewing key terms and concepts and applying them to your life as a citizen.

The Practice Tests and the Learning Outcomes   Now look at the two practice tests in the back of the book. Following the exact format of Ohio's Citizenship Proficiency Test, each practice test consists of 50 multiple-choice questions. Every test question relates directly to one of the 17 learning outcomes. Care has been taken to distribute the questions among the outcomes exactly as the state directs. For every learning outcome, a practice test includes no less than two and no more than five items relating to that outcome.

Taking a test is a skill in itself. To help you get ready for the proficiency test, we have suggested some tips and test-taking strategies (pages 141–143) that should help you to do your best on the day of the exam.

Why does Ohio require every student in the state to pass a proficiency test in four areas: reading, writing, math, and citizenship? The state government wants to make sure that the high school diploma you receive represents a certain level of learning in critically important areas. By reading the chapters in this book, completing the exercises, and taking the practice tests, you will acquire the knowledge and skills that you need to pass a major test. Even more important, you will know enough as a "proficient citizen" to understand how our democratic system of government works and how you can participate in the civic life of your community, your state, and your nation.

J. Mark Stewart
James A. Norris

The Seventeen Learning Outcomes in Citizenship

To demonstrate proficiency in citizenship, students must be able to:

1. Identify the major significance of the following historic documents: Declaration of Independence, Northwest Ordinance, U.S. Constitution, and Bill of Rights.
2. Know that many different peoples with diverse backgrounds (cultural, racial, ethnic, linguistic) make up our nation today.
3. Identify various symbols of the United States: flag, national anthem, Pledge of Allegiance, and Independence Day.
4. Locate the United States, the nation's capital, the state of Ohio, and Ohio's capital on appropriate maps of the nation, hemisphere, or world.
5. Demonstrate map-reading skills, including finding directions, judging distances, and reading the legend.
6. Know the following economic concepts:
   a. All levels of U.S. governments assess taxes in order to provide services.
   b. Individuals and societies make choices to satisfy wants with limited resources.
   c. Nations become interdependent through trade.
7. Identify major economic systems: capitalism, socialism, and communism.
8. Distinguish the characteristics, both positive and negative, of various types of government: representative democracy, monarchy, and dictatorship.
9. Demonstrate an understanding of the concept of federalism by identifying the level of government (local, state, national) responsible for addressing the concerns of citizens.
10. Identify the main functions of each branch of government (executive, legislative, judicial) at the national, state, and local levels.
11. Describe the process for making, amending, or removing laws.
12. Understand that the major role of political parties in a democracy is to provide a choice in governmental leadership.
13. Understand the role of officials in government.
    a. Distinguish between elected and appointed officials.
    b. Describe the ways officials can be elected or appointed.
    c. Evaluate the actions of public officials on the basis of a given set of criteria.
14. Know how the law protects individuals in the United States.
    a. Give examples of rights and freedoms guaranteed in the Bill of Rights.
    b. Apply the concept of justice,

including due process and equity before the law.

c. Know the importance of a learning or work environment free of discrimination against individual differences.

d. Identify legal means of dissent and protest against violation of rights.

15. Know that voting is both a privilege and a responsibility of U.S. citizenship.

a. Recognize that property ownership, race, gender, literacy, and certain tax payments no longer affect eligibility to vote.

b. Identify the qualifications for voting.

16. Demonstrate the ability to use information that enables citizens to make informed choices.

a. Use more than one source to obtain information.

b. Identify points of agreement and disagreement among sources.

c. Evaluate the reliability of available information.

d. Draw conclusions by reading and interpreting data presented in charts and graphs.

e. Identify and weigh alternative viewpoints.

17. Identify opportunities for involvement in civic activities.

NOTE: The learning outcomes listed here are identical in content to the state of Ohio's official list. The sequence of outcomes has been changed, however, to enable you to study related topics together. For example, both learning outcomes in the text dealing with economics (outcomes 6 and 7) follow right after each other instead of being separated.

CONTENTS

SKILLS EXERCISES

1

Historic Documents

LEARNING OUTCOME: Identify the major significance of the following historic documents: Declaration of Independence, Northwest Ordinance, Constitution, and Bill of Rights.

In a massive stone building in Washington, D.C., two documents are on display in tightly sealed cases of glass and bronze. One document, the Declaration of Independence, is a single sheet of vellum (calfskin) with words elegantly written in ink. At the bottom are the signatures of American revolutionaries—John Hancock, Thomas Jefferson, Benjamin Franklin, and others. At the top is the document's title, which looks like this:

IN CONGRESS. JULY 4, 1776.

The unanimous Declaration of the thirteen united States of America,

In a separate case beneath the first document are the several pages that make up a second document entitled "The Constitution of the United States of America." People pause in front of the case to admire this document's famous first paragraph:

Millions of visitors to our nation's capital have stood in long lines in the National Archives Building to see the two most famous and important documents in U.S. history. Why are they so important? What do these documents say? After reading this chapter, you will know the main ideas contained in the *Declaration of Independence* and the *U.S. Constitution.*

You will also become familiar with two other famous documents that were written about 200 years ago. The *Northwest Ordinance* of 1787 guaranteed certain liberties to early settlers north and west of the Ohio River. The *Bill of Rights* has defined the rights of all U.S. citizens ever since it became part of the U.S. Constitution in 1791. How did these documents come to be written? What do they mean to us today? In this chapter, you will discover the answers.

We the People of the United States, in order to form a more perfect Union, establish Justice, insure domestic Tranquility, provide for the common defense, promote the general Welfare, and secure the Blessings of Liberty to ourselves and our Posterity, do ordain and establish this Constitution for the United States of America.

1

The Declaration of Independence

Parades, fireworks, and backyard cookouts are all familiar parts of a Fourth of July celebration. It is easy to forget that the Fourth of July celebrates a past event of great importance. On July 4, 1776, a group of Americans representing different colonies approved the Declaration of Independence. In doing so, they announced their decision to form a new nation—the United States of America.

Why the Document Was Written Why was the Declaration of Independence written? Recall that, before 1776, Great Britain had 13 colonies on the Atlantic coast of North America. Over time, ties between Britain and its colonies weakened. By the mid-1700s, many colonists thought of themselves more as Americans than as citizens of Britain. In 1765 and again in 1767, the British government placed a number of new taxes on items commonly bought in the colonies. Tea, for example, was taxed for the first time. In 1773, a group of angry citizens in Boston, Massachusetts, protested the new taxes by dumping 342 crates of tea into Boston Harbor. This event is now known as the Boston Tea Party. Britain then tried to punish Massachusetts by banning its town meetings and reducing the power of its elected representatives.

Residents of other colonies felt threatened by Britain's harsh actions against Massachusetts. In 1774, they sent representatives to a "congress," or meeting, in Philadelphia. This First Continental Congress urged each colony to prepare to defend its liberty against any further threats from Britain. Colonists gathered weapons and ammunition to arm volunteer troops, called *militias*.

Such activity was bound to result in violence. Early one April morning in 1775, British troops began a march from Boston to the nearby town of Concord. The troops were to seize a stockpile of colonial military supplies. When the troops passed through the town of Lexington, someone fired a shot. That shot led to fighting between British soldiers and American militiamen in Lexington, Concord, and elsewhere. An all-out war between Britain and its colonies now seemed likely.

In May 1775, a Second Continental Congress met in Philadelphia to organize a response to Britain's actions. At first, most members of this Congress did not favor the idea of independence. But as more battles were fought, they finally decided that the time had come to break away from British rule. In 1776, a committee of five was formed to write a formal announcement, or declaration, that the united colonies were to be free and independent. Thomas Jefferson of Virginia was the chief writer of the document. On July 4, 1776, Congress voted to approve his work—the Declaration of Independence.

What the Document Says Jefferson had written a powerful document. He explained why Americans were justified in rebelling against British rule. First, he outlined a theory of government consisting of these points:

◆ **All men are created equal.** (In other words, all human beings are born with certain God-given rights.)
◆ People are born, for example, with equal rights to **life, liberty, and the pursuit of happiness.** (By "pursuit of happiness," Jefferson meant a person's freedom to choose his or her own goals in life.)
◆ Government rules by **the consent of**

On April 19, 1775, some 70 Minutemen intercepted British troops marching through Lexington. It is not known which side fired first, but when the smoke cleared, eight colonists were dead and ten were wounded. (*The Bettmann Archive*)

the governed. (In other words, a government's laws are not legitimate unless they are approved by a vote of the people's elected representatives.)

◆ If a government fails to protect people's rights, **it is the right of the people to alter or to abolish it, and to institute new government.** (People have the right to revolt against a government that misuses its powers.)

After making these arguments, Jefferson listed specific actions of the British king, George III, that had violated Americans' rights. Among these actions were:

◆ **Quartering** [stationing] **large bodies of armed troops among us**

◆ **Imposing taxes on us without our consent**

◆ **Depriving us in many cases of the benefits of trial by jury.**

In his concluding paragraph, Jefferson declared that the former British colonies were now 13 independent states within a new nation, the United States. Jefferson argued that since the king had violated the colonists' natural rights, colonists had the right to declare their independence. They also had a legal right to run their own government.

The 56 signers of the Declaration recognized that they could lose everything if their war against British rule went badly. That is why they ended the document by pledging to each other "our lives, our fortunes, and our sacred honor." As you know, Americans then went on to win the Revolutionary War after a hard, seven-year struggle.

The Northwest Ordinance

While the war with Britain was still being fought, the 13 states adopted a plan of U.S. government called the *Articles of Confederation*. Ratified in 1781, the plan gave certain powers to a Congress made up of members representing the different states. One of Congress's most important actions was to conclude a peace treaty with Britain in 1783. By the terms of this treaty, the United States won its independence as a new nation. It also gained a large tract of land north and west of the Ohio River. This land was known as the *Northwest Territory* and included the area that was to become Ohio.

Why the Document Was Written   In the 1780s, American settlers were already streaming into the Northwest Territory in search of cheap land. How was this land to be governed? Could new states be made from it? A group of land investors called the Ohio Company urged Congress to provide answers.

Reverend Manasseh Cutler, a representative of the Ohio Company, traveled to New York City (then the nation's capital) to advise Congress. Partly because of Cutler's influence, Congress drew up and passed a law for governing the Northwest Territory. This law of 1787—the Northwest

STATES CREATED FROM THE NORTHWEST TERRITORY

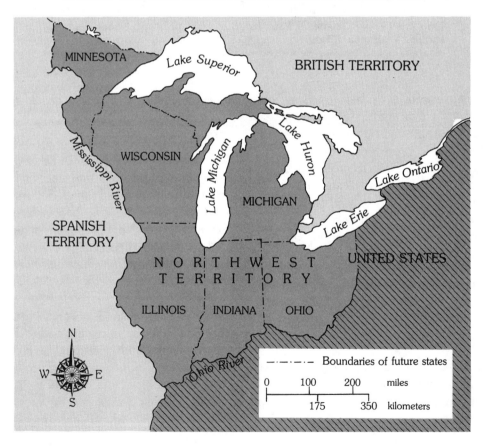

Ordinance—spelled out an orderly system of government for a newly settled U.S. territory.

What the Document Says The main points of the Northwest Ordinance were these:

1. Congress would appoint a governor, a *secretary* (high-level assistant), and three judges to serve as a government for the Northwest Territory. Laws for the territory could be "borrowed" from any laws already passed by one of the 13 states.

2. When the territory's population reached 5,000 adult males, an assembly could be formed. This assembly would consist of two houses. Members of one house would be appointed by the U.S. Congress. Members of the second house would be elected by the territory's adult, male settlers. The assembly could pass laws for the territory, but the governor would have to approve these laws. The assembly could also send a nonvoting delegate to the U.S. Congress.

3. A section of the Northwest Territory that had attained a population of 60,000 adult males could apply for statehood. If its application were accepted by Congress, the section would become a new state equal in status to the original 13 states. Eventually, five new states were created from the Northwest Territory. Ohio was the first, winning its statehood in 1803. The others were Indiana (1816), Illinois (1818), Michigan (1837), and Wisconsin (1848).

4. The Northwest Ordinance did more than create a workable system of territorial government. It also guaranteed certain liberties to people living in the territory. In fact, it listed many rights that were not yet guaranteed to people in the Eastern states. It read:

♦ **There shall be neither slavery nor involuntary servitude in the said territory, other than the punishment of crimes.** This ban on slavery in the United States was unique at the time. In the 1780s, most African Americans were held as slaves. (Only a small minority of African Americans at this time were free.) The Northwest Territory became the first part of the United States where slavery was *not* permitted.

♦ **No person. . .shall ever be molested** [punished or abused] **on account of his** [or her] **way of worship or religious sentiments.** In other words, all residents of the Northwest Territory were guaranteed freedom of religion.

♦ **The inhabitants of the territory shall always be entitled to the benefits of. . .trial by jury. . .[and] proportionate representation of the people in the legislature.** This statement guaranteed two rights that are basic to American democracy. The right to a "trial by jury" means that persons accused of crimes may defend themselves before a group of fair-minded citizens (the jury members). The right to "representation of the people in the legislature" means that voters may elect representatives to make laws on the people's behalf.

TEST YOURSELF

The following questions refer to information presented on pages 1–5.

1. (a) What was the Declaration of Independence? (b) Why are its ideas important to Americans today?

2. (a) What was the Northwest Ordinance? (b) What rights did it guarantee to the settlers of the Northwest Territory?

3. What is meant by the phrase "consent of the governed"?

The United States Constitution

Why the Document Was Written   A *constitution* is a plan for organizing a government and giving it powers. The first such plan for the U.S. government was the Articles of Confederation. The 13 original states gave their approval to this document in 1781. Soon afterward, it became clear to many American leaders, including Benjamin Franklin and George Washington, that the plan was not working. Under the Articles, Congress did not have enough power to govern effectively. It could not collect taxes or regulate trade between the states. Moreover, economic and political problems threatened to tear the new nation apart.

During the summer of 1787, delegates from 12 states met in Philadelphia to change the Articles of Confederation. (Rhode Island chose not to participate.) After the delegates had discussed the nation's problems, most of them decided that an entirely new constitution would be needed.

What Principles Are Included in the Constitution   The delegates who framed (wrote or created) the Constitution in the summer of 1787 have been called "founders" or "framers" of the Constitution. Although the delegates rejected the Articles as weak, they also feared that a national, or central, government might become too powerful. It might then take rights and freedoms away from ordinary citizens. Americans had recently fought the Revolutionary War to gain their freedom from British rule. They did not want to risk losing that freedom to an overly powerful U.S. government. For this reason, the framers wrote three main ideas into the Constitution: (1) federalism, (2) separation of powers, and (3) checks and balances. They believed that these principles (rules or standards) would produce a government whose power would be limited and under control.

Federalism is a form of government in which power is divided between a national government and state governments. Under the U.S. Constitution, the national government centered in Washington, D.C., has specific powers, such as printing money and making treaties with other countries. At the same time, the separate governments of the states have other powers, such as operating schools and building roads. Under this arrangement, no single level of government can gain all the power.

Most of the rules of the U.S. Constitution apply to just one government—the national government. (The separate state governments have their own constitutions.)

Separation of powers means that power is divided among three branches (or parts) of government. The branch with power to make laws is the *legislative branch*. In the U.S. government, lawmaking power belongs to Congress. A second branch, with power to enforce the laws, is the *executive branch*. In the U.S. government, the chief executive in charge of this branch is the president. A third branch, with power to operate the courts and interpret the laws, is the *judicial branch*. In the U.S. government, the Supreme Court is the most powerful of the many courts that make up the judicial branch.

The framers believed that by distributing powers among the three branches, no one branch could become too powerful.

Checks and balances means that each branch of government has ways of checking, or stopping, the actions and decisions of the other two branches. For example, a bill passed by Congress does not become a law until the president signs it. The president can disapprove of the bill by refusing to sign it. The bill is then said to be *vetoed*—stopped from becoming a law. Many such checks and balances are written into the Constitution. The framers included them to keep any one branch of government from becoming too strong.

How the Constitution Was Ratified In September 1787, after weeks of exhausting debate, the framers of the Constitution sent the document to the states for their approval. There were lively debates in each state about whether the proposed constitution should be *ratified* (approved). Those in favor of the document were called *Federalists*. Those opposed were called *Antifederalists*. Finally, in June 1788, the required number of states (nine) voted to ratify the Constitution. It then became the basis of our government. The Constitution has remained the "supreme law of the land" for more than 200 years.

How the Constitution May Be Amended The framers recognized that the nation would change over the years. They therefore wrote a document flexible enough to be adapted to new times. A part of their plan of government was to give Congress the power to propose *amendments* (formal changes or additions) to the Constitution. The states would then vote on whether to ratify a proposed amendment. So far, a total of 27 amendments have been added to the original documents.

TEST YOURSELF

The following questions about the U.S. Constitution refer to pages 6–7.

1. Define each of these terms: *amendment, constitution, federalism, separation of powers, checks and balances, ratify.*
2. Which powers of government did the Constitution assign to (a) the president, (b) the Congress, and (c) the federal courts?
3. Why is the U.S. Constitution supremely important to our system of government today?

The Bill of Rights

Why the Document Was Written Those who argued against ratifying the Constitution in 1787 and 1788 (the Antifederalists) pointed out a major weakness in the document. It did not include any list of the people's rights and freedoms.

Such a list is known as a "bill of rights." Supporters of the Constitution (the Federalists) agreed to add a bill of rights as soon as the Constitution was ratified. Consequently, one of the first acts of Congress after the Constitution took effect was to propose a set of amendments. The ten amendments ratified by the states in 1791 came to be known as the Bill of Rights.

What the Document Says The Bill of Rights protects the liberties that Americans have come to take for granted. The First Amendment guarantees freedom of speech, freedom of the press, freedom of religion, and freedom of assembly (meeting in a group). Other amendments in the Bill of Rights guarantee fair procedures by the police when arresting suspects and a fair trial for the accused. Each amendment protects the rights of U.S. citizens by saying what government *cannot* do. For example, officials of the U.S. government cannot:

◆ pass a law that favors a particular religious group
◆ prevent a religious group from worshipping in its own way
◆ punish someone for expressing an opinion

- ◆ punish someone for printing an opinion
- ◆ require a homeowner to give lodging to soldiers
- ◆ search or seize private property without a judge's warrant (written permission)
- ◆ punish someone for a crime in "cruel and unusual" ways
- ◆ compel persons accused of crimes to testify against themselves during trials.

POINTS TO REMEMBER

1 The Declaration of Independence (adopted by Congress on July 4, 1776) announced to the world that the 13 American colonies of Great Britain were forming a new and independent nation, the United States. The document declares that all people are born with rights to "life, liberty, and the pursuit of happiness."

2 The Northwest Ordinance (adopted by Congress in 1787) created a method for governing territory outside the boundaries of the original 13 states. It explained how new states (including the future state of Ohio) could come into being. Most important, it guaranteed rights to the settlers of the Northwest Territory and prohibited slavery in that region.

3 The U.S. Constitution (drafted in 1787 and ratified by the states in 1788) describes the basic plan of government of the United States. It divides powers among three branches of government. It creates a federal system in which some powers belong to the national government, while other powers belong to the various state governments.

4 The Bill of Rights (ratified by the states in 1791) is another name for the first ten amendments to the U.S. Constitution. It guarantees freedom of religion, freedom of speech, the right to a jury trial, and other basic rights to all U.S. citizens.

EXERCISES

CHECKING WHAT YOU HAVE READ

A. Read the following statements about the Constitution. On your answer sheet, write *F* if the statement is a *fact*. Write *O* if the statement is an *opinion*. (See the discussion of facts and opinions on pages 123–124.)

____ 1. The United States Constitution is the best plan of government in the world.

____ 2. Twenty-seven amendments have been added to the Constitution.

____ 3. The Constitution makes it too easy for criminals to escape arrest and prosecution.

____ 4. After 1791, the Bill of Rights was part of the Constitution.

____ 5. The Constitution gives each branch of government the power to check the other branches.

____ 6. The Constitution has given the president too much power.

____ 7. Thomas Jefferson wrote most of the Declaration of Independence.

____ 8. As the legislative branch, Congress makes the nation's laws.

____ 9. The Bill of Rights should have outlawed slavery.

____ 10. Failure to list people's rights in the original Constitution of 1787 was a bad mistake.

B. On a separate piece of paper list the numbers 1–12. For each of the numbered descriptions, write the letter(s) of the correct historic document(s).

a. Declaration of Independence   c. United States Constitution
b. Northwest Ordinance   d. Bill of Rights

_____   1. Outlawed slavery in a U.S. territory
_____   2. The basic framework, or plan, of the federal government
_____   3. The first ten amendments to the U.S. Constitution
_____   4. Listed colonists' grievances against King George III
_____   5. Established the three branches of the U.S. government
_____   6. Announced that the United States was a new nation
_____   7. Guarantees freedom of speech and the press
_____   8. Serves as the "supreme law of the land"
_____   9. Provided the first government for settlers of present-day Ohio, Indiana, Illinois, Michigan, and Wisconsin
_____   10. Stated that "all men are created equal"
_____   11. Guarantees a fair trial for all citizens
_____   12. Provided a process for territories to become states

USING WHAT YOU HAVE READ

On a separate sheet of paper, copy the following chart. Complete the chart by comparing the rights and privileges guaranteed in the Northwest Ordinance with those guaranteed in the Bill of Rights.

COMPARING TWO HISTORIC DOCUMENTS

Rights and Privileges in the Northwest Ordinance	Rights and Privileges in the Bill of Rights	Rights and Privileges in Both Documents

THINKING ABOUT WHAT YOU HAVE READ

Imagine that the year is 1776 and you are a reporter for a Philadelphia newspaper. You have just learned about the signing of the *Declaration of Independence*. Write a brief news article that explains to your readers the who, what, when, where, and why of the Declaration.

SKILLS: ORDERING EVENTS

During what period of time did Americans create the four historic documents described in this chapter? You might answer: about 200 years ago, during and right after the American Revolution. But how far back in time was that? It is hard to imagine a span of 200 years. . .or 100 years. . .or 50 years. Time lines like the one below help us to visualize the flow of time from past to present. They also show the sequence in which events occurred and how much time passed between one event and another.

SELECTED EVENTS IN U.S. HISTORY

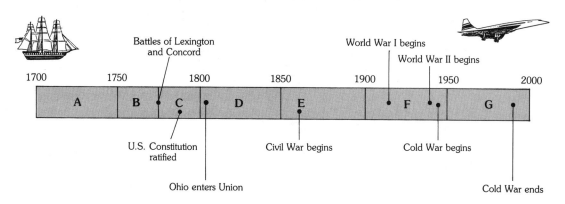

Referring to the time line, answer questions 1–10 on a separate sheet of paper. Question 10 asks you to create a time line of your own.

1. How many years in all are represented by the time line?
2. How many years are represented by the letter *A*?
3. What years are represented by the letter *C*? (Give the starting date and end date.)
4. Which letter represents the period during which you were born?
5. Which letter represents the period during which the United States was "born" (by being declared independent of Great Britain)?
6. Which *two* letters represent the colonial period *before* the American Revolution?
7. Which letter represents the period during which the U.S. Constitution and the Bill of Rights were written?
8. Which letter represents the period during which Ohio was admitted as a new state?
9. Which *five* letters represent the period during which the U.S. Constitution has served as the "supreme law of the land"?
10. Create a time line about six inches long. On the top of the line, mark the following dates: 1750, 1760, 1770, 1780, 1790, 1800. Allow an equal length of the time line for each decade. Copy the following events on your time line, placing each one close to the year when it took place.

    ◆ Signing the Declaration of Independence
    ◆ Passing the Northwest Ordinance
    ◆ Ratifying the U.S. Constitution
    ◆ Adding the Bill of Rights to the Constitution.

2

Cultural Diversity

LEARNING OUTCOME: Know that many different peoples with diverse backgrounds (cultural, racial, ethnic, linguistic) make up our nation today.

If you visit the Statue of Liberty in New York Harbor, you will find at its base a poem written by Emma Lazarus in 1883. The poem concludes with these famous words:

> Give me your tired, your poor,
> Your huddled masses yearning to
>   breathe free,
> The wretched refuse of your teeming
>   shore.
> Send these, the homeless, tempest-
>   tost to me.

> I lift my lamp beside the golden
>   door!

Both the statue and the poem symbolize the freedom and opportunity of living in the United States. Both celebrate the fact that people from all over the world have adopted the United States as a place to live. Throughout our nation's history, millions of women and men have come here from abroad as *immigrants*. These newcomers as well as their children and grandchildren have helped to make the United States a strong nation.

Native Americans

The first people to settle in North America were the Indians, or Native Americans. Originally an Asian people, they emigrated to this continent some 20,000 to 40,000 years ago during an *ice age* (a period when the world's climate was cooler than today's). As they spread across the North American continent, different groups of Native Americans invented a rich variety of languages and cultures. Each culture took shape in response to the demands of the natural environment. Woodland cultures in the East therefore were quite different from cultures on the Western plains.

The earliest Native American people to settle in Ohio lived in prehistoric times thousands of years ago. Indians known as the Hopewell people created huge burial

11

and ceremonial mounds, some of them in the shape of animals and geometric figures. Eventually, for reasons that are still unclear, the culture of the mound-building Hope-

wells died out. Other Native American peoples took their place. Among these Indians of Ohio were the Erie, the Miami, the Shawnee, the Wyandot, and the Delaware.

Colonial Times

Europeans became interested in exploring North and South America after Christopher Columbus's famous voyages in the 1490s. The Spanish and the Portuguese were the first Europeans to establish permanent settlements in the "New World." Early Spanish settlements were formed in Mexico, Florida, and a region that would later become the southwestern part of the United States. The English and the French began to colonize the Atlantic coast of North America in the early 1600s.

Reasons for Immigrating   The first European immigrants had several motives for coming to America. Some wanted to find gold and silver. Others wanted to teach Christianity to the Native Americans. Still others wanted the freedom to practice their own religion. (In many parts of Europe, there was no religious freedom. A government would establish one official religion and then tolerate no others.) Later, many immigrants came for economic opportunities. They wanted good land for farming or a chance to prosper at some trade or craft.

By the mid-1700s, Great Britain had established 13 colonies on the eastern shore of North America. Immigrants arriving in

colonial times brought with them the customs and languages of their native countries. The English were in the majority, but they were only one of many ethnic groups that immigrated to Pennsylvania, New York, and the other colonies. Thousands of others came from every part of Europe, including Germany, France, Ireland, Scotland, Sweden, Denmark, Switzerland, and the Netherlands.

Africans   One group of people did not come to the British colonies by choice. They were the Africans who had been captured and enslaved by other Africans and then traded as slaves to European ship captains. Shipped to the British colonies, most of these Africans remained in bondage for the rest of their lives. Their children and grandchildren were also treated as the property of colonists. In the colonial era, enslaved Africans managed to endure extreme hardships.

As time passed, some owners allowed their slaves to become free. Whether living in a state of slavery or in freedom, African Americans developed their own distinctive culture, which they passed on to later generations.

Immigration to a Growing Country

Western Lands   After the United States declared its independence from Britain in 1776, the nation grew rapidly. Indian lands

in the West attracted both native-born settlers and foreign-born immigrants. The West of the 1780s and 1790s was the

Northwest Territory, a region between the Ohio River and the Mississippi River. It included what later was to become the state of Ohio. In 1788, Rufus Putnam established at Marietta the first permanent, non-Indian settlement in the Northwest Territory.

From its earliest frontier days, Ohio was settled by a variety of ethnic groups. French settlers founded the town of Gallipolis, a name that means "city of the French." Another sizable group, the Moravian Germans, settled in northeastern Ohio. Most early settlers in Ohio were of English heritage.

The United States continued to expand westward in the 1800s. The country doubled in size in 1803 when it bought from France a huge Western territory—the Louisiana Purchase. In 1848, lands formerly under the control of Spain and Mexico came under U.S. rule after the Mexican War ended in a U.S. victory. Mexicans living on these Western lands now became

U.S. citizens. The California Gold Rush of 1849 brought waves of prospectors to California mining towns around San Francisco. Some of the prospectors came from a variety of foreign lands, including China, Australia, South America, and Europe.

Peak Years of Immigration   The last half of the 19th century (1850 to 1900) brought tremendous growth and change to U.S. society. The nation was becoming industrialized. New factories employed many workers who had previously worked on farms. Also coming to the cities to fill the thousands of new factory jobs were immigrants from Eastern and Southern Europe. By 1900, U.S. cities that exceeded 100,000 people included the Ohio communities of Cincinnati, Cleveland, Columbus, and Toledo. In the early 1900s, nearly one million immigrants came to the United States each year.

The new immigrants came mainly from countries of Eastern and Southern Europe,

In July 1788, the first capital of the Northwest Territory was set up at Marietta, on the Ohio River. While Native Americans had long lived in Ohio, Marietta became the first permanent white settlement there. (*Ohio Historical Society*)

These immigrants from Europe were among the more than 12 million people who crossed the Atlantic between 1890 and 1920. (*The Byron Collection, Museum of the City of New York*)

including Poland, Hungary, Italy, Greece, Austria, Slovenia, Croatia, Romania, and Russia. They brought with them a mixture of religions, including Judaism and the Roman Catholic and Eastern Orthodox forms of Christianity. The different ethnic groups founded their own foreign language newspapers, restaurants, and shops. At the same time, they struggled to learn English and the unfamiliar ways of their adopted land. Some observers thought that the United States was becoming a *melting pot*—a society of different ethnic groups who were adopting a common culture.

As U.S. territory expanded, so did the number of groups included in the U.S. population. In 1898, the Pacific islands of Hawaii became part of the United States. Also in that year, a war with Spain ended with the United States acquiring other island territories—the Philippines, Guam, and Puerto Rico. The different cultures of these islands were added to the large mix of cultures that then made up U.S. society.

Changes in the Immigration Laws

Congress has the power to regulate immigration. In the 1920s, many native-born Americans felt suspicious of foreigners and wanted to cut back the number of immigrants who would be allowed into the country. In 1924, Congress passed a law placing tight limits, or quotas, on immigration from the nations of Eastern and Southern Europe. Further immigration from Asia was banned altogether.

Congress changed the immigration laws again in 1965. It reopened opportunities for Asians to come to the United States. More immigrants from Latin America and Eastern and Southern Europe would also be admitted under the new law. Because of this change in the law, most immigrants arriving in the United States since 1980 have come from Asian countries (such as China, Vietnam, India, Taiwan, South Korea, and the Philippines) and from Latin American countries (such as Mexico, Cuba, and Guatemala).

Like the immigrants who preceded them, today's immigrants have come to the United States for two reasons: (1) religious and political freedom and (2) economic opportunity. In coming here, they are contributing their own cultural ways and individual talents to our amazingly diverse nation.

Evidence of Cultural Diversity

Whether they have come from Africa, Asia, Europe, Australia, or Latin America, immigrants have brought with them the customs of their original homelands. They practice different religions, prepare foods in different ways, and enjoy different kinds of music, games, and sports. They do not abandon their cultural ways upon arriving in this country. Instead, each immigrant group adds their customs to the life of the cities and farms where they have settled.

Diversity in the Cities   On the streets of a city like Cleveland or Columbus, we see signs all around us of the diverse cultures that make up American society. There are Presbyterian churches (originally founded by Scottish settlers), Jewish synagogues and temples (originally founded by Polish, Russian, and German immigrants), Buddhist temples (founded by Chinese and other Asians), Greek Orthodox churches (founded by Greeks), Roman Catholic churches (founded chiefly by Irish and Italians), Islamic mosques (founded by Arabs and African Americans), . . . and so on. Ohio cities have Chinese, Mexican, Indian, French, German, and other ethnic restaurants. Ethnic neighborhoods preserve some of the ways of their immigrant past.

For example, the Romanian Folk Museum on Cleveland's west side exhibits Romanian rugs, ceramics, religious objects, embroidery, and other crafts.

On the radio and TV, we hear popular songs in both Spanish and English. The rhythms of jazz and rock and roll come out of the musical traditions of Africa and African Americans.

Ohio's Cultural Heritage   As you travel the roads and highways of Ohio, you come upon many signs of *cultural diversity*. The Indian heritage of the state is well preserved in Ross County. Here you could visit burial mounds of the Hopewell culture, a Native American people who lived in Ohio hundreds of years before the time of Christopher Columbus. In the same area, you could go to Sugarloaf Mountain Amphitheatre to see *Tecumseh,* an award-winning dramatic production. Tecumseh, a leader of the Shawnee nation in the early 1800s, tried to unite Indian peoples of the Northwest Territory in a grand alliance against the white settlers.

German Village near downtown Columbus is a reminder of the thousands of German immigrants who came to the area in the 19th century. It is one of the largest privately financed historical restorations in the United States. Brick streets are lined with quaint shops and small brick homes built in the early and middle 1800s. Each autumn, the German Village Society sponsors an Oktoberfest, a celebration of German food, music, dancing, and culture.

Continuing your travels in central Ohio, you might pass through Holmes County, where a large number of Amish people live. The Amish, originally from Switzerland, are successful farmers whose religion teaches them to reject modern machinery and modern forms of dress. Most Amish use horses and buggies as their only means of transportation. Tourists flock to the Amish towns of Charm, Berlin, and Millersburg to purchase quilts and other traditional Amish crafts and to dine in Amish restaurants.

Heading south and west from Millersburg, you might stop in Greene County to visit Wilberforce University. Founded more than 100 years ago, in 1856, Wilberforce was one of the first universities to be established by and for African Americans. Nearby is the National Afro-American Museum, which celebrates the cultural heritage and achievements of African Americans.

These are just a few examples of Ohio's rich cultural diversity. Through the 1990s, the state's population will probably become even more diverse as immigrants from many lands move to Ohio and adopt it as their home.

E Pluribus Unum   Immigrants of the past and the present are responsible for our nation's cultural diversity. Just as important, immigrants willingly adopted most aspects of the culture that they found when they arrived in this country—the common culture of the American people.

Muslims from Turkey, Jews from Poland, Buddhists from China, Roman Catholics from Mexico, Protestants from Norway, and hundreds of other religious and ethnic groups have all gone through a similar process. They learned the customs and values of their adopted country. They learned about the U.S. political system and its guarantees of equal rights for all. They learned to speak a common language (English), to dress in the American fashion, to celebrate various American holidays, to vote in American elections, to play American games and sports, and so on. In time, they valued the common American culture more than the separate cultures into which they had been born. Each individual, no matter what his or her national origin, was proud to say "I am an American."

On the back of a one-dollar bill, you will find the motto: "E pluribus unum." This Latin phrase means: one out of many. Out of many different peoples and cultures has come just one nation—the United States.

POINTS TO REMEMBER

1 Millions of people living in the United States today have ancestors who came here from other parts of the world.

2 From colonial times to the present, immigrants have come to this country in search of economic opportunity and political and religious freedom.

3 U.S. culture is a blend of many different cultures. Examples of this cultural diversity can be found in the variety of American religions, foods, and forms of music and recreation.

EXERCISES

CHECKING WHAT YOU HAVE READ

All of the following statements are true. Two statements express the main idea (*M*) of this chapter's learning outcome, while the other statements present facts (*F*) that support the main idea. For each statement, write either *M* or *F*.

1. Native Americans are descended from an Asian people who came to North America tens of thousands of years ago.
2. The United States has always been a nation of immigrants.
3. The U.S. Congress changed the immigration laws in 1965.
4. As a result of immigration, many different peoples with diverse cultural and ethnic backgrounds make up our nation today.
5. Most of those immigrating to the United States in the 1980s were from Asia and Latin America.

USING WHAT YOU HAVE READ

Every time we sit down to eat, we benefit from the contributions of immigrant groups who have introduced their foods and cooking styles to the American diet. See if you can guess the ethnic origin of each of these foods.

1. spaghetti
2. sauerkraut
3. tacos
4. goulash
5. chocolate
6. Peking duck
7. tortillas
8. maize (corn)
9. pizza
10. crepes (dessert pancakes)

THINKING ABOUT WHAT YOU HAVE READ

Reread Emma Lazarus's poem on page 11. Then answer the questions below.

1. What phrases did the writer use to describe the immigrants?
2. The poem's last line states: "I lift my lamp beside the golden door!" What is meant by this line?
3. Emma Lazarus wrote this poem in 1883. Do you think it describes current U.S. policy toward immigrants? Explain.

SKILLS: INTERPRETING A TABLE AND A PIE CHART

Every year, an agency of the U.S. government—the U.S. Immigration and Naturalization Service—gathers information about the number of immigrants arriving from different countries and regions of the world. Its information can be presented in columns of numbers, such as in the table below. The same information can also be presented in visual, or graphic, form such as in a pie chart. Questions 1–5 below are based on both the table and the pie chart.

IMMIGRATION TO THE UNITED STATES, 1981–1990

Origin	Number (thousands)	Percent
Europe	761.5	10.4
Asia	2,738.1	37.3
North and South America	3,615.6	49.3
Africa	176.8	2.3
Other*	45.4	0.7

* Includes Australia, New Zealand, and islands of the Pacific Ocean

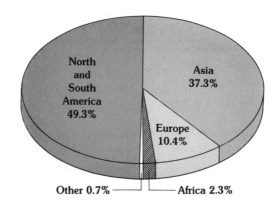

1. The largest number and percentage of immigrants to the United States in the 1980s came from (a) Europe (b) Asia (c) North and South America (d) Africa.
2. What percentage of total immigration in the 1980s came from Europe? (a) less than 15 percent (b) about 25 percent (c) about 50 percent (d) more than half
3. The number of African immigrants to the United States in the 1980s was (a) 2.3 thousand (b) 2.3 million (c) 1,768 (d) 176,800.
4. What information in the table is repeated in the pie graph? (a) the total number of immigrants from each region (b) the percentage of immigrants from each region (c) both the total number and the percentage of immigrants from each region (d) the percentage of Mexicans and Canadians who immigrated in the 1980s
5. Evidence from both the table and pie graph could be used to show that (a) people of European origin dominate U.S. society (b) newcomers to the United States represent different cultures (c) cultural diversity in this country is likely to decline in the future (d) Asian immigrants do not get along with South American immigrants.

3

National Symbols

LEARNING OUTCOME: Identify various symbols of the United States: the flag, the national anthem, the Pledge of Allegiance, and Independence Day.

What is a nation? It is *not* just a large piece of land defined by certain boundaries on a map. Besides the land, a nation consists of all the people living on the land and their customs and institutions. It also involves the feelings of common pride and loyalty that citizens have when thinking of their country. People express such feelings through the use of flags, songs, holidays, and other national symbols. Every citizen of the United States therefore should have some knowledge of those symbols.

The American Flag

"Old Glory" and "Stars and Stripes" are familiar nicknames for the official flag of the United States. This flag is a symbol that represents the nation. Whenever people see the "Stars and Stripes," they know that it stands for the United States of America.

Origins In the early months of the Revolutionary War, Americans fought under several different flags. Congress finally decided that a single U.S. flag was needed. On June 14, 1777, Congress passed a resolution saying that the official flag of the United States would have ". . . 13 stripes, alternate red and white; that the Union be 13 stars, white in a blue field, representing a new constellation." They chose the number 13 to represent the original 13 states that then made up the nation.

It is not certain who designed and made the first U.S. flag. According to popular legend, however, Betsy Ross made the first flag with red and white stripes and a blue square to show off the stars.

Nor is it certain what the colors on the flag stand for. But in 1782, Congress chose the colors for another national symbol—the Great Seal of the United States. It stated that the *red* on this design stood for hardiness and courage; *white,* for purity

19

and innocence; and *blue,* for vigilance, perseverance, and justice.

The Great Seal of the United States

Today's Flag Every time a new state was added to the Union, a new star was added to the flag. For example, when Ohio joined the Union in 1803, it became the 17th state, and the U.S. flag that year bore 17 stars. Today's flag has 50 stars representing the 50 states that now make up the nation. The number of stripes, 13, has never been changed.

A U.S. citizen should know several rules for displaying or flying the flag. At one time, the flag could be flown outdoors only between sunrise and sunset. Congress removed this restriction in 1976 to permit the flag to be displayed both day and night. The flag should be flown at half-staff (halfway up the pole) on Memorial Day until noon. It should be flown at half-staff on other days to commemorate the death of a nationally known public official. The flag should never touch the ground. If it is hung on a wall, the field of stars should be to the viewer's left. On three occasions, citizens should remember to honor the flag by holding their right hand over their heart: (*a*) when the flag passes by in a parade; (*b*) when it is present during the playing of the national anthem; and (*c*) when the Pledge of Allegiance is recited.

Thirteen-star flag, 1777

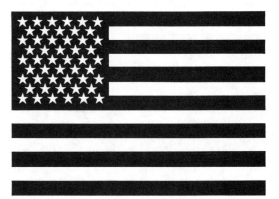

Fifty-star flag, today

The National Anthem

At major sporting events, it is the custom for Americans to stand up and sing these familiar words:

Oh! say, can you see, by the dawn's
    early light,

What so proudly we hailed at the twi-
    light's last gleaming?
Whose broad stripes and bright stars,
    thro' the perilous fight,
O'er the ramparts we watched were
    so gallantly streaming?

And the rockets' red glare, the bombs
  bursting in air,
Gave proof thro' the night that our
  flag was still there.
Oh! say, does that star-spangled banner yet wave
O'er the land of the free and the home
  of the brave?

Origins This patriotic song, *"The Star-Spangled Banner,"* was written by a lawyer and amateur poet, Francis Scott Key, in September, 1814. The United States was then at war with Great Britain—a conflict called the *War of 1812* (because the war had begun in that year). Key was on a ship in Baltimore harbor when he wrote his most famous poem. The words "perilous fight" and "rockets' red glare" describe the violent event that he had just wit-

nessed—the shelling of Fort McHenry by British ships. Despite a savage bombardment that lasted nearly all day and all night, American forces survived and continued to hold the fort. Key wrote a poem in four stanzas to express his excitement that "our flag was still there." A few days later, a Baltimore actor sang the poem to the tune that we all know today as "The Star-Spangled Banner." (The melody of that song was used earlier in an old English drinking song and an American military march.) Key's original poem and borrowed melody quickly became popular.

"The Star-Spangled Banner" did not become the official national anthem until many years later—in 1931. In March of that year, Congress passed the National Anthem Act, which designated Key's song as the official anthem of the United States.

The Pledge of Allegiance

In classrooms across the United States, students begin the day by pledging allegiance to their nation's flag.

I pledge allegiance to the flag of the United States of America and to the Republic for which it stands, one Nation under God, indivisible, with liberty and justice for all.

Meaning of the Pledge To make a pledge is to make a solemn promise, or oath. A flag represents a nation. So by pledging allegiance (loyalty) to the flag, a person is actually pledging allegiance, or loyalty, to the nation for which the flag stands.

In giving "The Pledge of Allegiance," a citizen pledges loyalty not only to the flag but also "to the Republic for which it

stands." A *republic* is a nation with a democratic, or popularly elected government. Furthermore, the pledge makes two other points: (1) that the United States is indivisible (cannot be divided) and (2) that liberty and justice is guaranteed to all U.S. citizens.

Origins "The Pledge of Allegiance of the United States of America" was written by Francis Bellamy, an editor of a magazine called *The Youth's Companion*. The pledge was first recited in 1892, the year that marked the 400th anniversary of Columbus's first voyage to the Americas. President Benjamin Harrison wanted schoolchildren to recite the pledge as a patriotic gesture. In 1942, Congress officially inserted the pledge into the rules for the use of the flag. The words "under God" were added in 1954.

Independence Day

During the summer months, the most widely celebrated holiday in the United States is *Independence Day*—or the Fourth of July. It occurs on July 4th because on that date in 1776 Congress voted to approve the Declaration of Independence. As you know from Chapter 1 (page 2), the Declaration announced to the world that the 13 states from New Hampshire to Georgia were no longer colonies of Britain. They declared themselves free and independent states, and the United States, a free and independent country. In effect, when we watch fireworks and enjoy parades on Independence Day, we are having a birthday party for our nation.

POINTS TO REMEMBER

1 As a symbol, the American flag stands for the United States. U.S. citizens demonstrate their loyalty for their country by showing proper respect for the flag.

2 The U.S. national anthem is "The Star-Spangled Banner." Francis Scott Key wrote the words to the anthem during the War of 1812.

3 In reciting "The Pledge of Allegiance," a citizen promises to be loyal to the nation for which the flag stands.

4 Independence Day commemorates the decision on July 4, 1776, to declare the United States to be an independent nation.

EXERCISES

CHECKING WHAT YOU HAVE READ

A. On a separate sheet of paper, number 1–8. For each numbered phrase, write the letter of the correct national symbol.

a. United States flag
b. National anthem

c. Pledge of Allegiance
d. Independence Day

____ 1. An oath of loyalty
____ 2. A national birthday party
____ 3. Written after a battle
____ 4. "Old Glory"
____ 5. Words by Francis Scott Key
____ 6. The celebration of a historic document of 1776
____ 7. A promise of "liberty and justice"
____ 8. Includes a symbol for each of the 50 states

B. On a separate sheet of paper, number 1–8. Write *F* if the statement is a fact or *O* if the statement is an opinion.

——   1. Independence Day is more important than any other holiday.
——   2. The stars on the United States flag represent states.
——   3. Nobody should be allowed to burn a flag for any reason.
——   4. The Pledge of Allegiance states that the United States is a republic.
——   5. The national anthem is too hard for many people to sing.
——   6. The words of "The Star-Spangled Banner" were written during the War of 1812.
——   7. Every school day should begin with the reciting of the Pledge of Allegiance.
——   8. Congress approved the Declaration of Independence on July 4, 1776.

USING WHAT YOU HAVE READ

1. The Declaration of Independence states:

   We hold these truths to be self-evident, that all men are created equal, that they are endowed by their Creator with certain unalienable rights, that among these are life, liberty and the pursuit of happiness.

   Compare this statement to "The Pledge of Allegiance." Do you see any similarity between ideas in the Declaration and ideas in the Pledge? Explain.
2. In what way do the stars and stripes on the U.S. flag symbolize the meaning of federalism? (Review Chapter 1, page 6.)

THINKING ABOUT WHAT YOU HAVE READ

Do you think a citizen who wishes to protest some government policy has the right to burn a U.S. flag? Some argue that flag-burning is an act of free speech protected by the First Amendment to the Constitution (review page 7). Do you agree or disagree with this argument? Write your answer in the form of a "letter to the editor." Be sure to state your position and explain your reasons for taking that position.

SKILLS: ANALYZING A DOCUMENT

Rarely do Americans hear anything but the first stanza of Francis Scott Key's patriotic poem and song. There are actually four stanzas in all, printed below. Read the document and then answer the questions that follow.

THE STAR-SPANGLED BANNER

I

Oh! say, can you see, by the dawn's early light,
    What so proudly we hailed at the twilight's last gleaming?
Whose broad stripes and bright stars, thro' the perilous fight,
    O'er the ramparts we watched were so gallantly streaming?

And the rockets' red glare, the bombs bursting in air,
  Gave proof thro' the night that our flag was still there.
Oh! say, does that star-spangled banner yet wave
  O'er the land of the free and the home of the brave?

II

On the shore, dimly seen thro' the mist of the deep,
  Where the foe's haughty host in dread silence reposes,
What is that which the breeze, o'er the towering steep,
  As it fitfully blows, half conceals, half discloses?
Now it catches the gleam of the morning's first beam,
  In full glory reflected, now shines on the stream.
'Tis the star-spangled banner. Oh! long may it wave
  O'er the land of the free and the home of the brave!

III

And where is that band who so vauntingly swore
  That the havoc of war and the battle's confusion,
A home and a country should leave us no more?
  Their blood has washed out their foul footstep's pollution.
No refuge could save the hireling and slave
  From the terror of flight or the gloom of the grave,
And the star-spangled banner in triumph doth wave
  O'er the land of the free and the home of the brave.

IV

Oh! thus be it ever when freemen shall stand
  Between their loved home and the war's desolation,
Blest with vict'ry and peace, may the Heav'n-rescued land
  Praise the Pow'r that hath made and preserved us a nation.
Then conquer we must, when our cause it is just,
  And this be our motto—"In God is our trust."
And the star-spangled banner in triumph shall wave
  O'er the land of the free and the home of the brave.

1. The second to last line of each stanza refers to the   (a) glare from the sun   (b) coming of dawn   (c) fluttering U.S. flag   (d) country's military might.

2. In the first stanza, the author says he could see the flag during the night because of   (a) sea breezes   (b) moonlight   (c) spotlights   (d) light from explosions.

3. In the second stanza, the author says he could see the flag at dawn, despite the mist and fog, because of   (a) rockets' red glare   (b) sea breezes   (c) moonlight   (d) spotlights.

4. In the third stanza, second line, the author uses the word "havoc," which means   (a) advantage   (b) destruction   (c) finality   (d) plenty.

5. In the fourth stanza, the author is saying that   (a) God was on the Americans' side   (b) luck was with the British   (c) the Americans were doomed to defeat   (d) war is wrong.

4

Locating Places on a Map

LEARNING OUTCOME: Locate the United States, the nation's capital, the state of Ohio, and Ohio's capital on maps of the nation, hemisphere, or world.

Where in the world is the state of Ohio? How much do you think you know about the places that surround the state? Test yourself by answering the following six questions. (If you wish, you could seek the answers by referring to the maps in this book.)

1. In what hemisphere is Ohio located: the Western Hemisphere or the Eastern Hemisphere?
2. What body of water forms Ohio's southern border?
3. Which body of water is located farthest from Ohio? (a) the Atlantic Ocean, (b) the Pacific Ocean, or (c) the Mississippi River?
4. Is Ohio located closer to (a) the state of Florida or (b) the state of Texas?
5. Which lake forms most of the northern border of Ohio?

6. Is our national capital (Washington, D.C.) located closer to (a) Mexico City or (b) San Francisco?

(Answers to the mini-quiz are at the bottom of page 33.)

Knowledge of geography is important to our lives as citizens. We need to have a general idea of where continents and countries are located in order to follow what is happening in the news. When a news story is about Canada, for example, we should instantly picture in our minds a large country on the northern border of the United States. When a news story takes place in Peru, we should instantly think of a country on the west coast of South America, a few thousand miles to the south of Ohio. Anyone can acquire this kind of knowledge by studying various maps, including the ones in this chapter.

25

Locating North America on a World Map

Shapes You can recognize a friend's face whether you are looking at it from close up or from a distance. Similarly, you should be able to recognize your continent, North America, whether it is shown with other continents or by itself. Compare Map 1 below with Map 2 on page 28. What are the chief differences between these maps?

One difference is in the way the island of Greenland is drawn. Notice that on Map 1 Greenland appears larger than the United States. On Map 2, however, the same island appears to be only about one-fourth the size of the United States. Why is this? The reason is that the earth is round like a ball, while a map is flat like a pancake. When a ball with some picture on it is flattened out, the picture will get stretched out of shape. The same thing happens when a mapmaker tries to create a map of the world. The mapmaker chooses a method for representing a three-dimensional area on a flat surface. The several methods for doing this are known as *projections*. On most map projections, the shapes of land areas close to the North Pole and the South Pole become stretched. That explains what happened to Greenland, Alaska, and northern Canada on Map 1.

A *globe* (small-scale model of the Earth) has the shape of a ball. Therefore, the land areas on every part of a globe can be drawn without distortion. If your classroom has a globe, find Greenland on it and observe this island's true shape and size. Then compare Greenland on the globe with Greenland on Maps 1 and 2. Which map gives a better (more accurate) view of this land area?

Even though the extreme upper and

MAP 1: THE WORLD

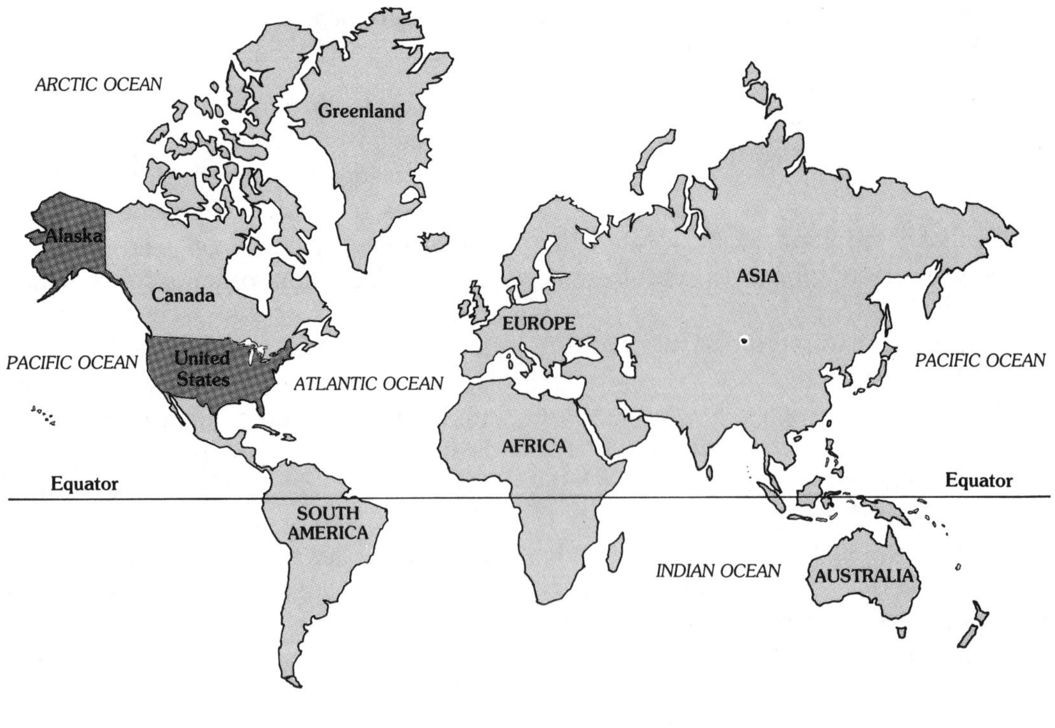

lower parts of Map 1 are distorted, you should have no trouble recognizing the different continents.

Relative Location Suppose that all the labels on Map 1 (the names of continents and oceans) were removed. Would you be able to locate North America by remembering where it is? To do so, you would use what geographers call a place's *relative location*. North America's relative location is its position on the map relative to other places. On a world map, you would locate North America by noticing the continents and oceans that surround it. You would observe the following:

◆ As its name suggests, North America lies north of the imaginary, world-circling line known as the *equator*. Also, naturally enough, it is north of the continent of South America.
◆ North America lies between the world's two largest oceans—the Atlantic Ocean to the east (right side of the continent) and the Pacific Ocean to the west (left side of the continent).

Notice that North America and South America are connected to each other by a thin strip of land (the Isthmus of Panama). Both are separated from the other continents by the Atlantic and Pacific Oceans. Together the two American continents are referred to as the *Western Hemisphere*. They are "western" in the sense that they lie to the west of Europe, the continent where at one time most maps were made.

TEST YOURSELF

The following questions refer to information presented on pages 25–27 and maps on pages 26 and 28.

1. Study the shape of North America on Maps 1 and 2 until you think you can remember what it looks like. Then close this book and draw the continent from memory. Now compare your map with Map 2. Then close the book again and draw North America a second time to see if you can improve your drawing.

2. In what direction is Africa located relative to (*a*) Europe, (*b*) the Atlantic Ocean, and (*c*) the Western Hemisphere?

Locating the United States and Ohio on Maps

Map 2 (on page 28) allows us to look at North America in some detail. We can locate the major nations of that continent (Canada, the United States, and Mexico) and Ohio. Once again, let us apply the method of locating a place by observing the places that surround it.

Relative Location of the United States Where is our nation relative to other nations? On Map 2, notice the following:

◆ The United States is located toward the center of the North American continent.
◆ The closest neighbors to the United States are (1) Canada, to the north, and (2) Mexico, to the south.
◆ The states of Alaska and Hawaii are separated from the other 48 states. Alaska is close to the eastern tip of Russia. Hawaii is in the middle of the Pacific Ocean.

Suppose you were presented with a blank (unlabeled) map of the world. What

MAP 2: NORTH AMERICA

method would you use to find the United States on such a map? You would probably first look for North America and then find the nation that stretches across the middle of that continent.

Relative Location of Ohio Where is Ohio in relation to the surrounding states and bodies of water? In looking for Ohio on a map, the first thing to do is to locate

the United States. Then find the five Great Lakes on the border between Canada and the United States. (Because of their huge size, these lakes are usually easy to find on a map of North America or the United States.) Next, of the five Great Lakes, look for the second one from the right, Lake Erie. Directly to the south of this lake is the state of Ohio.

Another way to recognize Ohio is to

memorize its distinctive shape. Notice that the state looks somewhat like a tulip blossom without the stem. On a piece of paper, try drawing Ohio from memory. Label the states and bodies of water that surround it: (*a*) Lake Erie, (*b*) Pennsylvania, (*c*) the Ohio River, (*d*) Kentucky, (*e*) West Virginia, (*f*) Indiana, and (*g*) Michigan.

Using a Grid to Locate Cities on Maps

A *capital* is a city where the highest officials of state or national government meet to make laws and govern that state or nation. As the capital of Ohio, Columbus is located almost exactly in the center of the state. As the capital of the United States, Washington, D.C., is located on the Atlantic coast about midway between the northern tip of Maine and the southern tip of Florida. The initials "D.C." stand for District of Columbia. Find both of these capitals on Map 3.

You can locate a city more easily if a map has numbers and letters running along its outside edges. Notice, for example, the numbers 1–5 and letters A–D on Map 3. Imaginary lines from these numbers and letters form a *grid* (a pattern of lines that cross at right angles). Each square or rectangular section formed by the grid may be identified by its letter and number. For example, we see on Map 3 that Columbus, Ohio, lies within section B–4.

What city is located within section B–5?

MAP 3: THE UNITED STATES (48 CONNECTED STATES)

POINTS TO REMEMBER ─────────────

1 To find North America on a map of the world, look for a large body of land located between two oceans. It is at the top, or northern, portion of the map.

2 To find the United States on a map of North America, look for a large, wide nation bounded mostly by an even larger country to the north (Canada) and a smaller and narrower nation to the south (Mexico).

3 To find Ohio on a map of the United States, look for the Great Lakes, and then for the tulip-shaped state just south of Lake Erie.

4 Columbus is in the center of Ohio. Washington, D.C., is located about halfway down the Atlantic coast of the United States.

EXERCISES

CHECKING WHAT YOU HAVE READ

All questions in this part refer to Map 4 on page 31.

1. What city is labeled *A* on the map?
2. Points *A, B, C,* and *D* are all located within what nation?
3. Which letter on the map represents the Great Lakes?
4. Which letter stands for the nation's capital, Washington, D.C.?
5. Which letter stands for a nation to the south of the United States?
6. Give both the name and letter of the only state indicated on the map.
7. City *B* is closest to what ocean?
8. City *D* is closest to what ocean?
9. If all of South America were also shown on Map 4, what would the total land area on the map be called?
10. What country lies directly north of the United States? (Give both its name and its letter.)

USING WHAT YOU HAVE READ

1. Select any state that borders on Ohio. Describe that state's relative location in terms of (a) the Great Lakes, (b) Canada, and (c) the Gulf of Mexico. (Refer to the map on page 28.)
2. Select any nation that borders on the United States. Describe that nation's relative location in terms of (a) the Atlantic Ocean, (b) the Pacific Ocean, and (c) the equator.

MAP 4: NORTH AMERICA

3. On a separate sheet of paper, draw an outline map of Ohio. Make a grid for your map similar to the one for Map 3 (page 29). Referring to an atlas, locate the following Ohio cities: Akron, Cincinnati, Cleveland, Columbus, Dayton, and Toledo. Place these cities on the map. Finally, just below the map, list the cities and give the sections in which they are located.

THINKING ABOUT WHAT YOU HAVE READ

1. Imagine that you are traveling in South America. Someone you meet asks what state you come from. "Ohio," you say. "Where's Ohio?" the person asks. How would you answer?
2. Write a paragraph describing the shape of North America. Write a second paragraph describing the shape of the United States.

SKILLS: USING LATITUDE AND LONGITUDE

In this chapter, you learned about Washington, D.C.'s relative location. Every city on Earth also has an *absolute location,* which is like the city's exact "address." The absolute location, or address, of Washington, D.C., is 38°N 77°W. Given this information, a skillful map reader would know that our nation's capital is located 38 degrees of latitude to the north of the equator. It is also 77 degrees of longitude to the west of the Greenwich meridian.

The map below shows how intersecting lines of latitude and longitude form a grid:

MAP 5: THE WESTERN HEMISPHERE

Lines of latitude are imaginary lines that run east and west around the Earth. They are always parallel to each other. The central line of latitude is the equator, which is given a value of 0°.

Lines of longitude are imaginary lines that run north and south across the Earth. They are never parallel. One line of longitude divides the Earth into two equal halves, or hemispheres. Because this line passes through Greenwich, England, it is called the *Greenwich meridian*. Like the equator, this line's value is 0° (longitude). Other lines of longitude are marked as so many degrees to the west of the Greenwich meridian (up to 180°W) and so many degrees to the east of that line (up to 180°E).

Practice your skill at locating places by means of latitude and longitude. Match each city in Column I with its absolute location in Column II.

I. Cities of the Western Hemisphere   II. Location

_____ 1. Rio de Janeiro, Brazil   a. 37°N 122°W
_____ 2. Santiago, Chile   b. 19°N 99°W
_____ 3. Mexico City, Mexico   c. 33°S 71°W
_____ 4. San Francisco, California   d. 41°N 82°W
_____ 5. Cleveland, Ohio   e. 22°S 43°W

Answers to mini-quiz on page 25:
1. Western Hemisphere
2. the Ohio River
3. b
4. a
5. Lake Erie
6. a.

5

Interpreting Map Symbols

LEARNING OUTCOME: Demonstrate map-reading skills, including finding directions, judging distances, and reading the legend.

Think of the road that passes in front of your school. If you make a right turn on that road as you leave the building, would you be facing north, south, east, or west? Or would you be heading somewhere in between these directions—either northeast, northwest, southeast, or southwest? Are you unsure of the answer? A map of your local area would tell you precisely which way you're heading—*if* you know how to read the map.

Now think of the distance you travel daily between home and school. Do you know how far it is between those points? Again a map would help you determine the an-

swer—*if* you know how to use it.

Imagine traveling by car from Akron to Cincinnati. Should you take an interstate highway or a two-lane state road or both? Looking at a road map would give you the answer—*if* you can read its legend.

Whether a map shows an area as large as a continent or as small as a city, it usually uses three devices that help you read the map. They are a: (1) compass rose for finding directions, (2) scale of miles and kilometers for judging distances, and (3) legend for identifying map symbols. This chapter will explain how to use all three of these map features.

Using a Compass Rose to Find Directions

Most of the time, though not always, maps are drawn so that north is at the top of the map frame. If north is at the top, then south is at the bottom, east is to the right, and west is to the left.

Compass Rose On the map of North America on page 35, notice the flower-like symbol in the map's lower, left-hand corner. This symbol is a *compass rose*. Its purpose is to indicate the exact directions of north, south, east, and west on a particular map.

The compass rose looks like the face of a magnetic compass. Have you ever held a compass in your hand and watched its needle swing toward true north—the North Pole? Suppose that you were lost in a forest but happened to have both a compass and a map of the forest's trails. To find the direction in which you are facing, you would simply line up the **N** point of the map's compass rose with the northward pointing needle of your compass.

On the map of North America, notice the line pointing toward **N** (north). Notice that the other *cardinal directions*—**S** (south), **W** (west), and **E** (east)—line up with the arrow. South is always in the opposite direction from north. West and east are always opposite each other, to the left and right of the north-south line.

Notice the smaller lines on the compass rose. They point to intermediate, or in-between, directions: northeast, southeast, northwest, and southwest.

Directional Arrow Sometimes, instead of the full compass rose, a map will have a *directional arrow*, like the one on Map 6 below. It points in one direction—north (N). Just by knowing where north is, you

MAP 6: OHIO AND NEIGHBORING STATES

can easily identify the other cardinal directions. (Remember that south is always directly opposite north. West is to the left of the north-south line, at a right angle. East is directly opposite west.)

Suppose you failed to look at the directional arrow on Map 6 and assumed that north lay at the map's top and center. You would then assume that Indianapolis lies to the north and west of Columbus, Ohio. But you would be wrong. Checking the directional arrow, you would see that Indianapolis lies directly to the west of Columbus—not to the northwest.

Using a Scale to Measure Distances

Suppose that you were taking a trip from Cleveland to Indianapolis and wanted to know the distance between these two cities. Referring to Map 6, you could determine the distance by referring to the map's scale of distance.

Scale of Distance The *scale of distance* is usually located at the bottom of a map. Often this scale is unlabeled and consists of just a horizontal line evenly marked off into units of distance (miles or kilometers or both). On Map 6, the scale represents a distance of 200 miles.

How do you use a map scale to determine distances? First, you place the straight edge of a scrap piece of paper just below the scale's horizontal line. With a pencil, you copy all of the vertical marks on the scale.

Next, you place your marked scrap of paper on the route between Cleveland and Indianapolis. Starting at Indianapolis, you place the edge of the marked paper along the route between the cities. Lightly marking the first 200 miles (the full length of the scale), you move the scale to the right one more time until it reaches Cleveland and beyond. You find that the distance is the length of one full scale (200 miles) plus part of a length more (70 miles). You conclude then that the trip to Indianapolis will be approximately 270 miles.

Practice the skill of using a map scale by carrying out all of the above steps.

TEST YOURSELF

Use the scale of distance and the directional arrow on Map 6 to answer the following questions.

1. What is the distance between Columbus, Ohio, and Washington, D.C.? (*a*) about 200 miles (*b*) about 250 miles (*c*) about 320 miles (*d*) about 500 miles

2. An airplane flying directly from Cleveland to Detroit would travel how many miles? (*a*) about 50 (*b*) about 100 (*c*) about 150 (*d*) about 200

3. Cleveland is located (*a*) almost directly west of Columbus (*b*) almost directly west of Frankfort, Kentucky (*c*) almost directly north of Charleston, West Virginia (*d*) south and east of Washington, D.C.

4. A car leaving Indianapolis would travel how far and in what direction if its destination was Columbus? (*a*) about 100 miles going east (*b*) about 100 miles going south (*c*) about 175 miles going east (*d*) about 175 miles going north

MAP 7: SMITHVILLE AND JONESVILLE

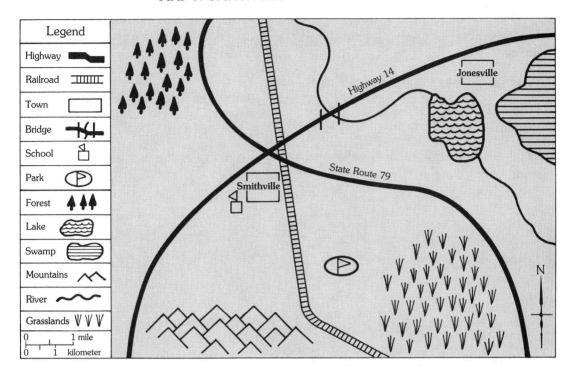

Using a Map Legend

Let's look at a different kind of map. Map 7 is a road map of an area near the imaginary towns of Smithville and Jonesville.

In the northwest (top left) corner of the map, we see a number of the same symbols bunched tightly together. In the southeast (bottom right) corner, we see another bunch of symbols. What do these and other symbols represent? The answers are given in the *legend* to the left of the map.

Legend This map feature—also called a "key"—presents a list of every symbol on the map. Next to each symbol is the name of the thing that it represents. For example, we see from the legend for Map 7 that the treelike symbols in the northwest corner

represent a forest; the grasslike symbols in the southeast corner represent grasslands.

The legend to a map is like the caption to a picture. It explains what you are seeing. Many maps would be almost impossible to interpret if they had symbols but no legend.

TEST YOURSELF

Use the legend to Map 7 to answer the following questions.

1. What building lies just outside Smithville?

2. What body of water cuts across Highway 14?

3. What is located between the grasslands and the railroad track?

4. What symbol is used to indicate a bridge?

5. What road lies to the north of the lake?

6. What town lies to the west of the railroad?

7. What lies just east of Jonesville and south of Highway 14?

POINTS TO REMEMBER

1 When using a map to determine direction, refer to the compass rose (or the directional arrow).

2 When using a map to determine distances, refer to the scale (of miles or kilometers). Copy the scale on a piece of paper and use it as a measuring device.

3 To interpret the symbols on a map, refer to the legend.

EXERCISES

CHECKING WHAT YOU HAVE READ

Tell whether you would use a compass rose, a scale, or a legend to solve each of the following problems:

1. On a map of Ohio, you want to find out how far Cleveland is from Toledo.

2. On a map of the United States, you want to find out whether Colorado is west or east of Utah.

3. On a map of a state park, you want to know where the camping areas are located.

4. On a map of the world, you want to estimate the distance in miles between New York City and Paris, France.

5. On a road map, you want to know whether Route 78 is a four-lane highway.

THINKING ABOUT WHAT YOU HAVE READ

Obtain a road map or other map that shows your community and surrounding area. Draw a simplified version of this map, showing only the *major* roads. Include a legend, a compass rose, and a scale of distance. Finally, write five to ten questions about your map like those for Map 7, page 37. Exchange maps and questions with a friend. You should answer your friend's questions; the friend should answer yours.

USING WHAT YOU HAVE READ

The following questions refer to Map 8 below. For each question, select the letter of the correct answer.

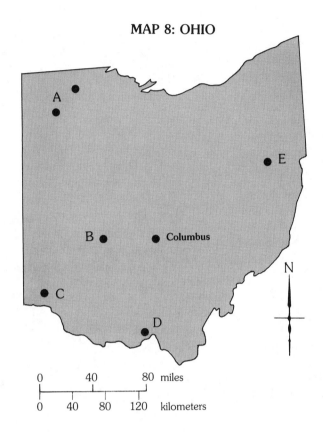

MAP 8: OHIO

1. If you went 40 miles west from Columbus, Ohio, where would you be? (a) C (b) A (c) E (d) B

2. From Columbus to point A, about how many miles is it? (a) 40 (b) 80 (c) 100 (d) 120

3. A truck traveling from Columbus to point A would be going in what direction? (a) due north (b) due west (c) northeast (d) northwest

4. A trip from Columbus to point B and then from B to C would be about how many miles? (a) 100 (b) 220 (c) 300 (d) 440

5. What is the direction and distance in traveling from Columbus to point D? (a) 160 miles south (b) 75 miles south (c) 220 miles north (d) 220 miles southeast

6. To go from point A to point C and then to point E is approximately how many miles? (a) 220 (b) 320 (c) 420 (a) 520

SKILLS: USING MAP LEGENDS

Study Map 9 below. It is a road map of Cincinnati and the surrounding area. Using the legend on this map, answer the following questions:

MAP 9: CINCINNATI

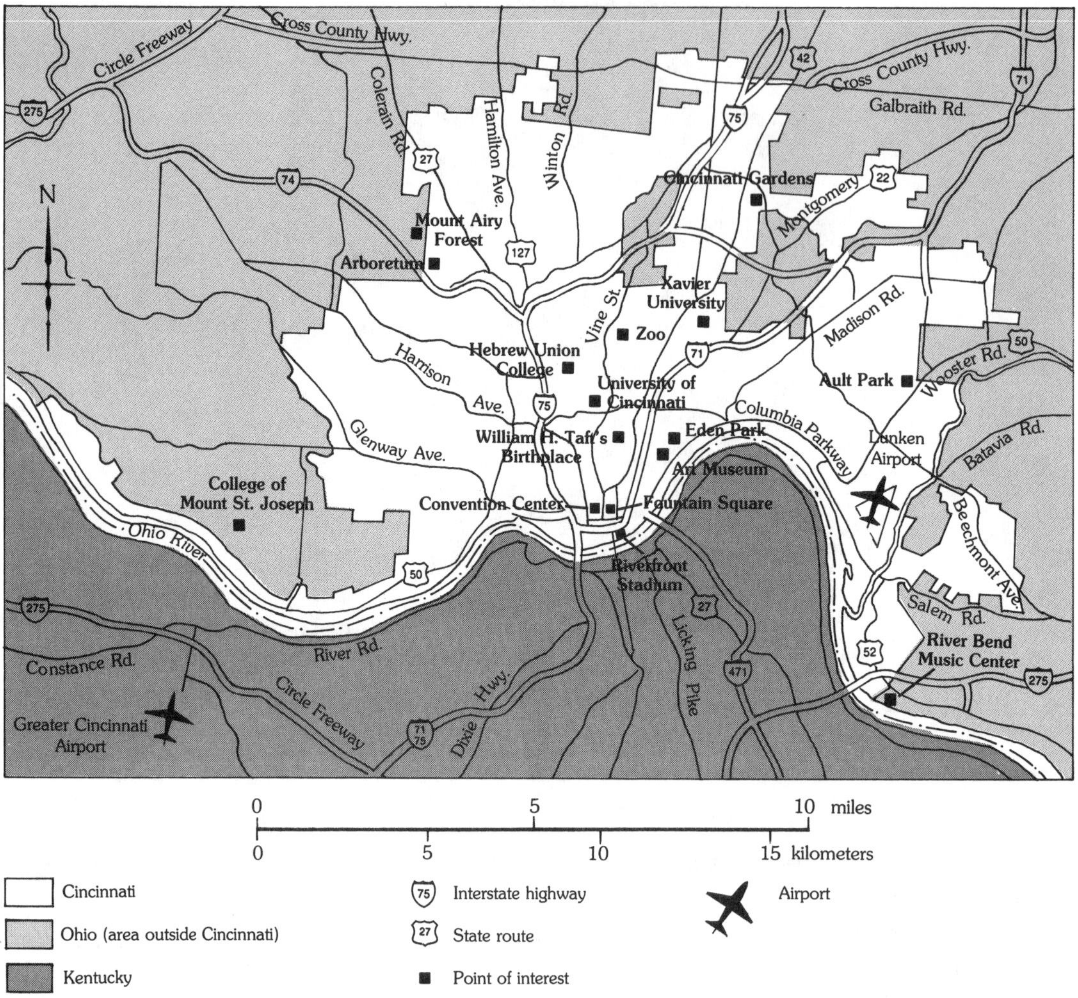

1. What are the numbers of the five interstate highways shown on the map?
2. Which state highway goes directly past River Bend Music Center?
3. The Greater Cincinnati Airport is located in what state?
4. If a driver left Lunken Airport and drove west on Columbia Parkway, what first two points of interest would she pass?
5. Suppose that you wanted to go from the Arboretum to Fountain Square. What major roads would you travel to get to your destination?

6

Economic Concepts

LEARNING OUTCOME: Know the following economic concepts:

a. Individuals and societies make choices to satisfy wants with limited resources.

b. All levels of U.S. government assess taxes in order to provide services.

c. Nations become interdependent through trade.

Economics is involved in almost everything that people do. Consider what you've done since waking up this morning. How many of the following activities have you already carried out? Did you . . .

◆ turn on an electric light?
◆ eat or drink something?
◆ spend money for something?
◆ ride in a car, bus, or other vehicle?
◆ receive instruction in math, English, history, or some other subject?
◆ use a TV set or radio?

These are all examples of *economic* activities because they all involve a cost of some kind. The use of electricity in a light bulb or TV set involves a cost (the use of the fuel and machinery needed to provide electric current). Eating food involves a cost—the price of whatever is eaten. Providing instruction in math, English, and history involves a cost because a teacher must be compensated, or paid, for time and effort.

Nothing that people do is free, or without cost. *Economics* is the subject that deals with this fundamental fact of human life.

In this chapter, you will learn how economics applies to your personal life in the decisions you make every day. You will also see how economics affects the nation (through taxes) and the world (through trade).

Choosing Among Limited Resources

Let us define a *resource* as anything that is useful or needed for attaining some goal. Think of the money in your pocket, wallet, or purse as one such resource. You know very well that your money supply is limited. Whether you are carrying $1 or $100, you know that it will eventually be spent. It will not buy everything you want. Your wants far exceed your limited means. You must, therefore, decide *how* to use your limited resource of $1 or $100, or whatever the actual sum is.

Unlimited Wants Think of all the things that you want now and will probably want in the near future. Does your list include a car? Clothes? A stereo system? A college education? Excellent health care? Keep extending the list, and you may discover that your wants are really endless. Even if your family is one of the richest in the world, you cannot afford to buy everything. You have to make choices—economic choices—now and throughout your life.

For a moment, stop thinking about your own limited resources. Stretch your imagination and try to think of all the resources on planet Earth. It has billions of acres of land, millions of farms, thousands of gold mines, silver mines, and oil wells, countless forests, lakes, and rivers, and on and on. Such vast resources may seem boundless. The fact is, however, that they are limited. There is only so much gold, so much oil, so much water, so much farmland, and so much rainforest. Somehow the more than five *billion* people who currently live on this planet must find ways to divide up the scarce resources available to them.

Scarcity The term *scarcity* is very important to economists. Scarcity simply means that people have unlimited wants, but that the resources to meet their wants are limited. Because resources are limited, people will always have to give up something to get what they want. Scarcity forces them to make economic choices.

AN ECONOMICS LESSON FOR POLLY

Opportunity Costs Think again about that money in your pocket, wallet, or purse. If you spend it for lunch, it cannot be spent for any other purchase. The real cost of spending money for a hamburger or soda is that it is not available for your countless other wants and needs. By choosing to spend a resource for one purpose, you lose an opportunity to spend it for other purposes. In other words, *every* economic choice that you make has an *opportunity cost*.

There are also opportunity costs for the economic choices that *every* society must make. Consider these choices, for example:

◆ Shall an acre of rainforest in Brazil be turned into an acre of farmland?

◆ Shall an acre of farmland in Ohio be turned into the parking lot for a shopping mall?

◆ Shall an old shoe factory in Massachusetts be torn down so that a new office building can be built in its place?

The same acre of land cannot be both rainforest and farmland at the same time. It can be used for one purpose or the other, not both. Therefore, a choice must be made. And each choice has a built-in cost—an opportunity cost. A cost of treating acre X as rainforest is that it is not available for farming. A cost of using acre X as farmland is that it ceases to be part of a rainforest. The opportunity cost of any choice is the lost opportunity to use the resource in a different way.

Goods and Services

Individuals are not the only ones who decide how scarce resources shall be used. Millions of businesses in the United States and around the world decide what *goods* (or products) shall be manufactured for sale. Certain businesses, for example, decide whether a factory shall make shoelaces or umbrellas, shaving cream or toothpaste, CDs or TVs. Other businesses provide *services* to customers. (A service is an economic benefit that comes directly from someone's labor. When you are served a meal at a fast-food restaurant, you are purchasing a service. When you go to a doctor for medical advice, a barber for a haircut, or a piano teacher for lessons, you are receiving that person's services.) Each business must decide what service or services to sell to consumers.

Governments also make economic choices involving both goods and services. The U.S. government, for example, decides whether or not to purchase new tanks for the army, new computers for its post offices, and new uniforms for its forest rangers. At the same time, state and local governments decide whether to purchase new textbooks for schools, new trucks for the fire department, new books for the library, new cars for the police, and new paving for the highways.

More important than the goods that governments buy are the services they provide. Police officers offer services to the public by keeping order and enforcing the laws. Teachers in the public schools provide educational services. People in the U.S. armed forces provide military services—protecting the nation from foreign dangers. Everybody employed by government is engaged in one way or another in serving the public welfare of the nation, the state, or the local community.

Government services often *appear* to be

given free of charge. The librarians in a public library give assistance without collecting a fee from book borrowers. A police officer charges no fee for directing traffic or helping a motorist in distress. A public school teacher collects no fee from students for teaching them how to read and write. As you know, however, every economic activity has a cost. Every cost must be paid by someone at som time in some way.

Paying for Government Ser es

Government charges the public for its many services by a method called *taxation*. It determines how much money it needs to pay all those employed in public services (the teachers, police officials, forest rangers, road engineers, sanitation workers, and so on). In order to pay the salaries of government employees (as well as other expenses), the government collects taxes from the citizens it serves. Before any tax can be collected, it must first be approved by a majority vote of the legislature.

Types of Taxes Taxes come in different forms. A *sales tax* is paid by consumers when they purchase items at a store. For example, when you buy a new sweater or jacket, you will have to pay a certain percent of the item's selling price as a state tax. That money goes to the Ohio government. A *property tax* is paid yearly by homeowners and businesses on the estimated value of their land and buildings. Property taxes pay most of the expenses of operating your local government.

An *income tax* is paid by anyone whose income for the year is above a certain amount. The national government gets most of its revenue (incoming money) from an income tax on individual wage earners and another income tax on corporations. Income taxes are also collected by Ohio and most other states.

A *Social Security tax* is a special type of tax collected by the U.S. government. Employers automatically deduct this tax from the paychecks of their workers. When an older worker retires from the work force, he or she is entitled to receive Social Security benefits in the form of monthly checks from the U.S. government.

TEST YOURSELF

The following questions refer to information on pages 41–44.

1. Define *opportunity costs* and give an example.

2. How does scarcity force everybody to make economic choices?

3. What economic choices are made by the government of Ohio?

4. Why are taxes necessary at all levels of government?

Trade in an Interdependent World

Think of five motorists pulling up to the pump at a gas station. The first driver happens to be a dentist. Behind her is the owner of a florist shop. Next comes a construction worker, then a high school teacher, and finally a waitress. All five customers depend on the gas station to supply them with one of their needs—fuel for their cars. At the same time, the gas station owner depends on the specialized services provided by her customers. She may need the dentist to fix her teeth, the florist to furnish flowers for a wedding, the construction worker to repair her driveway, the teacher to instruct her kids, and the waitress to serve her breakfast. She depends on their economic services; they in turn depend on being able to purchase gas from her st .tion.

Interdependence in the U.S. Economy

Those who depend on each other are said to be *interdependent*. In our economic lives, all of us are interdependent today. Either as business owners or jobholders, many of us specialize in delivering one kind of product or service. The money earned from our specialized labor gives us the opportunity, as consumers, to purchase the goods and services created by others. That is the way things work in a modern economy. We are so used to our interdependence as workers and consumers that we seldom think about it.

Interdependence in the World Economy

It is also becoming more and more obvious that nations of the world are interdependent. Economic survival for every nation depends upon being able to trade its goods and services for the goods and services of other nations.

To see why nations are interdependent, think of three imaginary countries: Treeland, Highland, and Agrica. As its name suggests, Treeland is covered by miles and miles of forests, but has few deposits of iron ore and coal. Highland is just the opposite—a mountainous land with a lot of coal and iron ore but not many trees. The third country, Agrica, is known for its large and fertile farms that produce bumper crops of wheat and many pigs. What would these three nations do to develop their economic strengths and make up for their economic weaknesses? Very likely, Treelanders would trade their timber to the other

INTERDEPENDENCE THROUGH TRADE

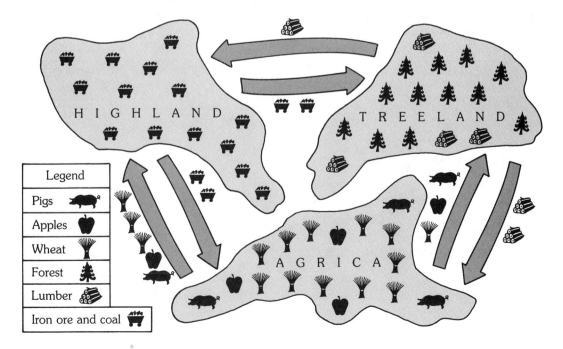

nations in return for Agrica's food and Highland's minerals. Agrica and Highland would be happy to make the trade since they both need Treeland's wood. Trade enables the economies of all three nations to prosper.

In a similar way, international trade is vital to the U.S. economy. Even though many of our needs can be satisfied by goods produced right here in the United States, other needs are better met by goods from abroad. U.S. businesses also need to be able to sell U.S. products to the people of other countries. For example, much of the food grown by U.S. farmers is sold abroad to those nations that lack enough farmland. At the same time, the United States imports coffee from Brazil, rubber from Indonesia, cameras and electronic equipment from Japan, oil from Saudi Arabia, automobiles from Germany, and minerals from all parts of the world.

To see how interdependent the world has become, try an experiment at home. Go through your home and identify as many items as you can that were manufactured, assembled, or grown in other nations. Look at the labels on your clothes. Also look at food, jewelry, appliances, and furniture. Keep a record of your findings. In one column, list those objects that were made or grown in the United States. In a second column, list foreign products and the nations where they come from.

POINTS TO REMEMBER

1 Scarcity of resources forces everybody to make economic choices.

2 Whenever you use a resource in one way, you automatically lose the opportunity to use the resource in other ways. This cost of every economic decision is known as an opportunity cost.

3 Governments provide a number of services, including police and fire protection, education, military defense, highway building and maintenance, and the delivery of mail.

4 The various taxes that citizens pay to the national, state, and local governments are needed to finance government services.

5 Trade among nations makes them interdependent.

EXERCISES

CHECKING WHAT YOU HAVE READ

On a separate sheet of paper, write the letter of the answer that best completes each statement.

1. Scarcity is an unavoidable fact of economic life because people have   (a) limited wants and limited resources   (b) unlimited wants and limited resources   (c) unlimited wants and unlimited resources   (d) limited wants and unlimited resources.
2. The opportunity cost of buying an umbrella for $20 is   (a) the lost opportunity to buy something else with the $20   (b) the cost of the umbrella plus an additional sales tax   (c) a cost shared equally by the manufacturer and the consumer   (d) a hidden cost of doing business in an interdependent world.
3. Government collects taxes to pay for all of the following *except*   (a) a forest ranger's services   (b) a teacher's services   (c) a police officer's services   (d) a department store's goods.
4. Both the U.S. government and Ohio's government collect   (a) a sales tax   (b) an income tax   (c) a Social Security tax   (d) a property tax.
5. When you purchase a watch made in Switzerland and a T-shirt made in Hong Kong, you are showing that the global economy   (a) has limited resources   (b) depends on government services   (c) depends on trade   (d) depends less and less on U.S. participation.

USING WHAT YOU HAVE READ

Why is each of the following an example of scarcity?

1. a homeless person whose wages are not sufficient to pay for both food and lodging
2. a millionaire whose bank account is not sufficient to support the purchase of either a third yacht or a fourth house
3. a government whose income from taxes is not sufficient to finance a college education for all qualified students

THINKING ABOUT WHAT YOU HAVE READ

1. Describe a day in your life *as if* you and the world at large had unlimited resources. What would you do with that day?
2. For three days, keep a record of the money you spend. For each item, record both the sales price and the sales tax. Then write an essay on *one* of the following topics:
   a. My opportunity costs in buying X, Y, and Z
   b. My recent contributions to government services in Ohio
   c. How I benefited from world trade.

SKILLS: INTERPRETING PIE CHARTS

The two pie charts below summarize where Ohio's state revenues came from and how they were spent in 1990. The questions 1–5 refer to the pie charts. For each question, write the letter of the answer that best completes the statement.

1. In 1990, the largest source of revenue for Ohio was the   (a) sales tax   (b) corporation income tax   (c) public utility tax   (d) personal income tax.

2. In 1990, Ohio spent the greatest amount of tax dollars on   (a) justice and corrections   (b) primary and secondary education   (c) human servic~s   (d) higher education.

3. Two taxes—the personal income tax and the sales tax—accounted for   (a) less than half the state's revenues   (b) about half the state's revenues   (c) about three-fourths of the state's revenues   (d) all but ten percent of the state's taxes.

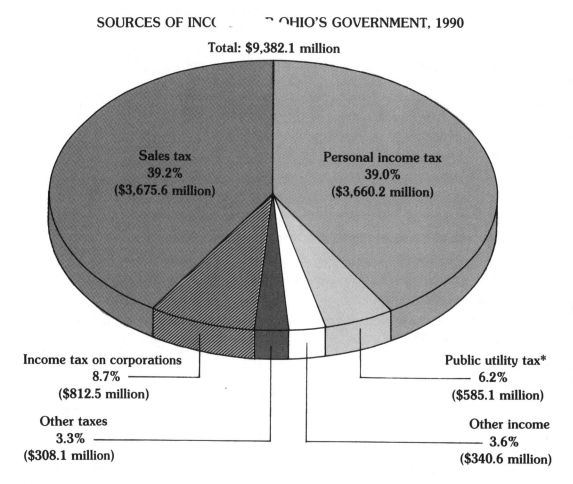

SOURCES OF INCC ⌐ ΩHIO'S GOVERNMENT, 1990

Total: $9,382.1 million

Sales tax
39.2%
($3,675.6 million)

Personal income tax
39.0%
($3,660.2 million)

Income tax on corporations
8.7%
($812.5 million)

Public utility tax*
6.2%
($585.1 million)

Other taxes
3.3%
($308.1 million)

Other income
3.6%
($340.6 million)

*A tax on companies that sell electricity, gas, and telephone services to the public

Source: Ohio Department of Taxation

4. Expenditures on all levels of education (primary, secondary, and higher) accounted for   (a) about one-quarter of the total   (b) about half the total   (c) about three-quarters of the total   (d) all but ten percent of the total.

5. Total expenditures in 1990 were   (a) equal to total revenues   (b) about $100 million less than total revenues   (c) about $100 million more than total revenues   (d) more than twice what was collected in taxes.

EXPENDITURES OF OHIO'S GOVERNMENT, 1990

Total: $9,489.5 million

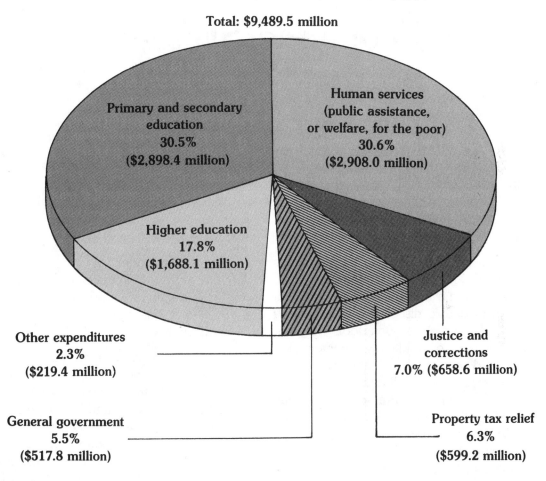

7

Economic Systems

LEARNING OUTCOME: Identify major economic systems: capitalism, socialism, and communism.

Imagine an abandoned factory that has been sitting idle and empty for many years. One day, on a hiking expedition, a small group of people discover the old factory and walk through its open door. They notice a number of hand tools hanging on the walls and power tools fastened to the workbenches. Stacked in all four corners of the factory's main room are scraps of metal, wood, cloth, rubber, and leather.

What's to be done with the factory, its tools and materials? Can the people who discovered these resources think of a plan for turning them into something useful and economically valuable? After discussing the problem among themselves, the group discovers that four main questions must be answered:

1. *What* should the factory produce?
2. *How and by whom* should the factory's products be made?
3. *How much* of products X, Y, and Z should the factory produce?
4. *To whom* should products X, Y, and Z be distributed?

These four economic questions must be answered by anyone who runs a business. Furthermore, these questions must be answered by *all* societies and *all* nations. As you learned in the last chapter, *every* nation has only a limited amount of resources. Ways must be found to convert those resources into goods and services. Which goods? Which services?

Every nation has developed an economic system that answers the four basic questions. The three systems most widely discussed and followed in the 20th century are (1) capitalism, (2) socialism, and (3) communism.

Capitalism

What are the basic principles of *capitalism*?

Private Ownership Let us suppose that the discoverers of the abandoned factory believe in capitalism. They will then look at the factory as a property that should belong to one owner or a group of owners. In other words, they will think of it as private property (not as public property that everyone in society owns in common). Capitalists think that factories, farms, stores, and other properties should be privately owned. They also believe that the owner or owners of each property should be free to decide what to do with the property.

Profit Motive Capitalists assume that the owners of a property like a factory or a farm would use it to make a *profit* for themselves. A profit is money left over after total costs are subtracted from total sales. In common speech, we say that a business "makes money," which is another way of saying that the business's income is more than its expenses.

Let us imagine what would happen to the abandoned factory if its discoverers bought the building and turned it into their private property. Under a capitalist system, they are free to use their resources (factory, tools, materials) in whatever way they think will bring the most profits. They could turn the old factory into a restaurant, a shopping mall, or a roadside inn. They could use the factory's tools and materials for manufacturing goods for sale. The new factory owners discuss ideas for making everything from an unbreakable flyswatter to a superior running shoe. They finally decide to make running shoes with distinctive blue soles. They call their new business the Blue Shoe Company.

Of course, the business owners need a labor force. They hire a group of workers, who are paid a certain wage (so many dollars per hour) for their labor. Unlike the owners, the workers receive none of the profits of the company (assuming it does make a profit). But the workers do not run the risk of losing an investment of money if the company should fail. In a capitalist system, business owners take the risk of loss as well as the reward of profit.

In a capitalist system, people may decide to invest in a corporation (or company) by buying *shares of stock* in that corporation. One share of stock is one share of ownership in the business. For example, the owners of the Blue Shoe Company might organize their business as a corporation and issue 1,000 shares of Blue Shoe stock. If there were ten owners who had invested equally in the company, each would own 100 shares. If the company makes a profit of $1,000 in the first year of business, each owner would be entitled to receive $100—one dollar per share.

Competition In addition to profits and private ownership, one other factor is crucial to a capitalist system. That is the role of competition. The Blue Shoe Company is not the only business to manufacture and sell running shoes. There is already a wide variety of these products sold by dozens of competing companies. The new company's shoes will succeed only if consumers prefer them to the shoes manufactured by others. In a capitalist system, competition in every industry forces a business to strive to create the best product or give the best service it possibly can. If the Blue Shoe Company fails to produce an excellent shoe that attracts thousands of buyers, the owners will go out of business.

Free Market Another name for capitalism is the *free market system*. It is "free" because the government does not control the system. Instead, thousands of private businesses decide independently what products and services they will attempt to sell to consumers. Consumers in turn are free to buy—or not to buy—the items offered for sale in the marketplace. Producers and consumers alike have freedom of choice.

TEST YOURSELF

The following questions refer to information on pages 50–52.

1. What are the basic characteristics of a capitalist system?

2. How does a capitalist system answer the question of *what* shall be produced?

Socialism

What are the basic principles of *socialism*?

Public Ownership Socialists argue that the *means of production* in society should be publicly owned, not privately owned. The means of production include everything people use to produce wealth (such as machines, tools, buildings, and land). Socialists want the means of production to

PROBLEMS OF A PLANNED ECONOMY

be owned and controlled by the government. Socialists believe that such a system would ensure fair wages and work hours for everybody. Also, workers would be almost certain to have steady employment because the government would be everybody's employer.

Government Planning Think again about the abandoned factory described at the beginning of this chapter. Suppose that instead of capitalists taking it over, the people who discover it are socialists. They would have an entirely different view of what to do with the factory. First of all, socialists would immediately ask the national government to take over the factory. They believe such resources should be used for the benefit of the entire society. Therefore, they argue, everybody in society should share equally in the ownership and control of economic resources. This can be accomplished, they say, by letting a popularly elected government own and run the nation's factories and farms.

Let us assume that a socialist government does take over the old factory. Would it be likely to use the building to produce items for sale and profit? No, a socialist government is not interested in profits. Its chief goal is to keep the total economy turning out the goods and services that are needed by society. It will try to fit the factory's output into the government's master plan for the total economy. For example, government planners may find that the factories assigned to making trucks do not have enough nuts and bolts. So they might order the old factory to manufacture nuts and bolts for the truck industry.

Communism

The basic idea of *communism* is closely related to socialism. Like a socialist system, a communist system is totally opposed to private ownership and profit seeking. Also like a socialist system, a communist system is, in theory, controlled by all the workers in society.

Marx's Theory To understand communism, you need to know something about the ideas of a German philosopher named Karl Marx. In 1848, Marx published a book called *The Communist Manifesto*. This book attacked the capitalist system and urged members of the working class to revolt against it. Marx predicted that workers all over the world would sooner or later join in a revolution. National governments would then be under the control of the workers and their political arm, the Communist party.

What would happen after the working class came to power and overthrew capitalism? According to Marx, the economic system would first go through a "socialist" stage and then pass naturally into a "communist" stage. During the socialist stage, the working class would have to use government and the laws to abolish the old capitalist system. For a while, all forms of productive property (factories, farms, stores, and so on) would be tightly managed by the government for the benefit of the workers. In time, however, the workers would have no more need for a government. Society would then enter into a final stage: communism. In this imagined society of the distant future, there would be:

◆ no social classes (no rich, no poor)
◆ perfect cooperation among all members of society (nobody competing for power, status, or wealth)

- ◆ equal distribution of goods and services so that everyone's economic needs are met
- ◆ ownership of productive resources by society as a whole.

When society entered this stage, Marx said, the state (government and laws) would *"wither away"* (disappear).

Marx died in 1883, but his theories about socialism and communism continued to be read and debated. Marx's ideas impressed thousands of workers who were unhappy about economic conditions in their countries. Believers in Marx's ideas were known as *Marxists.*

Communist Governments In the 20th century, Marxist revolutionaries managed to seize power in Russia in 1917, in China in 1949, and in Cuba in 1959. Russia changed its name to the Soviet Union. Here the Communist party took control, not only of the government but also of every other institution in society (such as factories, farms, stores, schools, newspapers, and movies).

Today, when Americans think of communism, we usually think of a political system as well as an economic one. It is a system totally under the control of a single political party—the Communist party. We think of harsh punishments and a secret police force that makes people afraid to speak freely on political issues.

Communists, in contrast, would define communism the way Karl Marx defined it. In their view, communism does not yet exist anywhere. It is a far-off goal, not a present reality. Communist leaders in China and Cuba would explain that their nations are currently in a socialist stage. Government, they claim, is still needed at this stage to protect the working class against capitalist enemies. When capitalism ceases to exist, then and only then will communism be possible (so say those who still belong to the Communist party).

The Economic Systems Today

So far, we have described "pure" systems that do not exist in reality. A pure capitalist system would be totally controlled by privately owned businesses. A pure socialist system would permit no privately owned businesses at all. In a pure communist system, all workers would cooperate for the common good of everyone without the need for a government.

In the real world, however, there is no nation whose economic system is all one thing or all another. Instead, every nation has some privately owned, capitalistic enterprises as well as some publicly owned, government enterprises. Take the United States as an example. Almost all of its factories, farms, and stores are privately owned and run as businesses for profit. At the same time, the U.S. government carries on many public enterprises such as delivering the mail across the country and supplying electric power to a region in the South (the Tennessee River Valley). Because *most* U.S. enterprises are privately owned, the U.S. economy may be called capitalist.

Take Sweden's economy as an example of *democratic socialism.* It is democratic in the sense that Swedish voters freely elect government leaders. It is partly socialistic because the government owns and operates several major industries, including the nation's railroads and electric power plants. At the same time, however, there are hundreds of privately owned, profit-seeking businesses in Sweden, including its world-famous Volvo and SAAB automobile companies. In theory, a socialist economy is one in which all the means of production are managed by the government. In reality, however, nations that we call "socialist" have only a few major industries that are government run. Other industries consist of freely competing, privately owned, profit-seeking businesses.

In the 1990s, socialism appears to be on the decline as an economic system. The Marxist form of socialism (what some people call "communism") is especially in trouble. In the past, the Soviet Union, East Germany, Hungary, and Poland tried to carry out Marx's theories. The factories and farms in these countries were all under government control. But then in 1990 and 1991, the Communist party lost power in Russia (the former Soviet Union) and the other countries of Eastern Europe. Today, these countries are trying to make the difficult transition to an economic system that is partly socialist and partly capitalist.

Examples of *Marxist socialism* ("communism") still exist in China, Cuba, North Korea, and Vietnam. In these countries, most factories and farms are under government ownership and control. Politically, people cannot freely choose their government leaders but must vote only for members of the Communist party.

It is now clear to most observers that Marxist socialism is a much less practical economic system than capitalism. The Soviet Union collapsed largely because its economy failed to produce enough goods and services to meet people's basic needs. Even in countries such as China, where the Communist party still rules, the government is allowing people to open up their own private businesses and sell goods and services for a profit.

POINTS TO REMEMBER

1 Every society must have a system for deciding what to do with its limited resources.

2 Capitalism is an economic system in which privately owned businesses compete with each other to sell goods and services for a profit.

3 Socialism is an economic system in which the government owns and operates the means of production (factories and farms) and takes complete control of the economy.

4 According to the theories of Karl Marx, communism is the final stage of socialism. A communist society would be one that had no need of government because workers' needs would be completely met without it. Defined in these terms, communism is only a theory—not a practical reality.

5 In the world today, no nation is purely capitalist or purely socialist.

6 Because most of its economic resources are privately owned, the U.S. economic system may be called capitalist. Even so, the U.S. government plays an important role in the economy by providing major public services, such as mail delivery.

EXERCISES

CHECKING WHAT YOU HAVE READ

For each numbered statement or descriptive phrase that follows, write

CAP if it describes the theory of capitalism
SOC if it describes the theory of socialism
COM if it describes Marx's theory of communism
ALL if it describes capitalism, socialism, and communism.

1. based on private ownership, competition, and free markets
2. answers the basic economic question of what society shall produce with its limited resources
3. depends on producers' desire for profits
4. puts the means of production under government control
5. practiced in the Soviet Union until 1991
6. places major stress on government planning
7. an idea never carried out in practice

USING WHAT YOU HAVE READ

1. Clip an advertisement from a magazine. Explain how this advertisement shows some of the characteristics of a capitalist economy.
2. (a) Define *means of production*. (b) Identify a piece of property in your local community that is an example of a means of production. (c) Tell how the use of this piece of property demonstrates capitalism at work.

THINKING ABOUT WHAT YOU HAVE READ

1. What strengths and what weaknesses do you see in capitalism?
2. What strengths and what weaknesses do you see in socialism?
3. Why do you think the planned economy of the Soviet Union failed to meet consumers' needs? After writing your answer, go to your school or community library and read about the fall of the Soviet economic system in 1991. Make a list of all the reasons you can find for its collapse. You might also ask your parents or other adults why they think the Soviet system failed.

SKILLS: COMPARING ECONOMIC SYSTEMS

Ever since the end of World War II, the Korean people have lived under two separate and hostile governments. Those living in North Korea have a government controlled by the Communist party. Most of North Korea's factories, farms, and other means of production are publicly owned. In contrast, Koreans living in South Korea have an economy in which most of the means of production are privately owned.

In short, North Korea practices socialism, while South Korea practices capitalism. Which system—the socialist system or the capitalist system—has succeeded better in producing various goods and services? The following statistics give some economic facts about the two Koreas. They are by no means the only relevant facts that can be used to compare national economies. As you examine the statistics, keep in mind that they give only a partial picture. Even so, you can still draw some conclusions about the economies of North and South Korea by comparing their production of steel, iron, TV sets, cars, and so on.

Study the data carefully. Then answer the questions based on it.

NORTH AND SOUTH KOREA, SELECTED DATA

	North Korea	South Korea
Population	22,937,000	42,793,000
Literacy Rate	99%	92%
Physicians	1 for every 379 persons	1 for every 1,139 persons
Hospital Beds	1 per 74 persons	1 per 487 persons
Death Rate per 1,000 Population	5.0	6.2
Average Annual Income per Household	$4,275	$11,530
Agriculture		
fish	1,800,000 tons	3,200,000 tons
rice	6,400,000 tons	8,200,000 tons
cattle	1,280,000	2,039,000
pigs	3,145,000	4,852,000
Manufacturing		
cement	8,200,000 tons	29,545,000 tons
crude steel	4,200,000 tons	19,198,115 tons
pig iron	5,800,000 tons	12,577,754 tons
chemical fertilizers	4,000,000 tons	3,814,864 tons
passenger cars	20,000	867,629
Communications		
TV receivers	250,000 (1 per 90 persons)	8,700,000 (1 per 4.9 persons)
telephones	10,000 (1 per 2,000 persons)	11,370,000 (1 per 3.7 persons)

Source: Adapted from "Britannica World Data," *Encyclopaedia Britannica Yearbook*, 1992.
(Note: Figures in each category were the most current available, 1988–1990.)

1. Which nation, North Korea or South Korea, has the larger population?

2. Which economy seems to have performed better in terms of each of the following?
   a. literacy
   b. health care
   c. average income
   d. agriculture
   e. manufacturing
   f. communications

3. When comparing two economies, is it better to compare (a) the total number of TV receivers and telephones or (b) the total number of an item divided by the total population? Why?

4. In general, which of Korea's economic systems—socialism or capitalism—seems to have produced more goods and services? Support your answer with several facts from the table.

5. Besides the facts in the table, what other information would help you compare the two Koreas' economies?

NORTH KOREA AND SOUTH KOREA

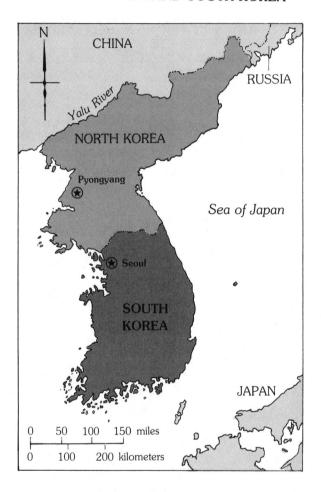

8

Types of Government

LEARNING OUTCOME: Understand the differences among three types of government: representative democracy, monarchy, and dictatorship.

Every nation has laws that people must obey. But the system for making and enforcing laws differs from one nation to the next. Consider some of the laws that you and other citizens must obey. In the United States, there are laws against:

- vandalizing property
- shoplifting
- robbing a bank or store
- causing deliberate harm to anyone
- driving recklessly
- throwing litter on the streets and highways

- failing to pay taxes.

These laws were *not* made by a king or a dictator. Who then has the authority to make the laws that we Americans are required to obey? In other nations around the world, what gives government officials their power both to make and to enforce laws?

In this chapter, you will learn about three systems for granting political power. You will learn how the U.S. system of representative democracy compares with other systems, such as a monarchy in Saudi Arabia and a dictatorship in Cuba.

Absolute and Limited Monarchs

Absolute Monarchs Centuries ago, most governments were headed by a single person—a monarch. The exact title of the monarch differed from one society to the next. There were kings and queens, emperors and tsars, sultans and pharaohs. What-

ever the title, it usually belonged to just one family—the royal family. A monarch's crown (the symbol of his or her power) passed down through the generations, usually to the monarch's eldest or most trusted son. An *absolute monarch* is a ruler who

59

Empress Catherine II (the Great) ruled Russia as an absolute monarch, 1762–1796. (*The Bettmann Archive*)

completely controls the government and its laws. The people either obey the monarch's laws or suffer harsh penalties for disobeying.

At the time of the American Revolution (the 1770s and 1780s), absolute monarchs governed most of Europe and much of the rest of the world. Since the 1700s, however, one royal family after another has been forced to surrender power.

A few monarchies do still exist. Examples of powerful monarchs in today's world may be found in the Middle Eastern nations of Kuwait and Saudi Arabia. A king rules in Saudi Arabia with almost total authority. He is the direct descendant of the first Saudi king, Ibn-Saud. As in most absolute monarchies, opposition to the king is not toler-

ated. Citizens are not free to speak out against the government. Nor can citizens take part in elections to choose public officials. All Saudi officials are appointed by the king, not elected by the people.

Limited Monarchs Not all monarchs have power that is total, or absolute. In Great Britain, for example, Queen Elizabeth II is a monarch whose power is extremely limited. She is a living symbol of the British nation and its long history and traditions. As such, the monarch serves to give stability to the British government and national pride to the people. In terms of real political power, however, Britain's monarch does little more than ratify (approve) the decisions of officials who are elected to office by the British people. The British type of government is known as a *limited monarchy,* or *constitutional monarchy.* In such a government, real power belongs to elected officials, not to the king or queen.

Advantages and Disadvantages of Absolute Monarchies Compared with other forms of government, an absolute monarchy has certain advantages. At its best, it can be a relatively stable form of government. People know that one person, the monarch, will continue to rule for the rest of his or her life. If the monarch is a capable leader and in good health, people are assured of the benefits of good government for many years.

On the other hand, when an absolute monarch dies, there can be much trouble over the question of who will be next on the throne. At the time of death, the appointed heir might be only a child. Ambitious persons then have an opportunity to challenge the prince or princess. Rival contenders for the throne might tear apart the kingdom in a bloody civil war.

Dictatorship

More common than monarchies in today's world are governments known as *dictatorships*. Unlike a monarch, a dictator does not sit on a royal throne or wear a royal robe and crown. Nor does a dictator usually inherit power from a parent. In one respect, however, dictators of modern times do resemble absolute monarchs. A dictator, like an absolute monarch, has total control of his or her nation's political system. No law can be passed without the dictator's approval. All officials in government take orders from the dictator.

How a Dictator Seizes Power   Someone seeking to become a dictator usually does so by means of military force. The person could be a high-ranking army officer who, for a time, pretends to be loyal to the existing government. Or the person could be a commander of rebel armies that are openly opposed to the government. We might call this military leader "The General." When he thinks he can get away with it, "The General" may declare a "national emergency" and announce that he is taking over the government. (If he is a rebel commander, his armies would have to defeat the government's forces.) "The General" would typically order his troops to arrest the top leaders of the old government. The new government organized by "The General" would be a military dictatorship.

How a Dictator Remains in Power
Once in office, the dictator usually pretends to be a great patriot and champion of the people. To show that the people support a dictator's government, elections may be held. But elections organized by a dictator are neither fair nor free. The ballot (list of candidates) usually gives only the names of loyal supporters of the dictator. The police

force under the dictator's control may use threats and actual force to stop anyone from saying anything against the dictatorship. Thus, the dictator and his or her party win election by a nearly unanimous vote time after time.

The island nation of Cuba is one country that has been ruled by a dictator for many years. The dictator, Fidel Castro, came to power in 1959 after a military defeat of the previous Cuban dictator. Castro and his supporters in the Communist party rule the nation without organized opposition. Many of Castro's opponents have been imprisoned. The Communist party is the only political party allowed in Cuba. Even though elections are held regularly, the Cuban people have no choice but to vote for the Communists that Castro picks for different

Italy's military dictator, Benito Mussolini, tightly controlled his country's government from 1922 to 1945. (*The Bettmann Archive*)

government jobs. There is an elected legislature, or lawmaking body. But it does nothing more than pass the laws that Castro wants.

Advantage of a Dictatorship   A dictatorship like Castro's may seem to Americans to be all bad because it deprives people of liberty, and rights are not guaranteed. But there is one main advantage to a dictatorship. When government is completely controlled by one leader, it can act quickly and decisively in an emergency. In the 1920s, for example, the Italian dictator Benito Mussolini came to the rescue of Italy's troubled economy by imposing his will on both business and labor. (Democracies, in contrast, are often slow to act in an economic crisis because disagreements among rival parties cause delays in passing laws.)

TEST YOURSELF

The following questions refer to information presented on pages 59–62.

1. How does an absolute monarchy differ from a limited monarchy?

2. In what ways does a dictatorship differ from an absolute monarchy?

3. What are one advantage and one disadvantage of a dictatorship?

Representative Democracy

The U.S. Constitution begins with these words: "We the people of the United States,. . .do ordain and establish this Constitution for the United States of America." The phrase "We the people" is very important. It means that U.S. citizens as a group ("the people") have the power to influence government and even to change the Constitution if they choose to do so.

Two Types of Democracy   The United States is a *representative democracy*. To understand this term, we first must know what democracy means. A *democracy* is a political system that gives the common people (average citizens) the opportunity to make laws for their own society. People who live in small towns may make laws directly by meeting perhaps once a month in the town hall. There they can decide by majority vote whether or not to approve a neighbor's idea for controlling traffic on Main Street, repairing a local bridge, or solving some other local problem. Town meetings are an example of *direct democracy.*

Unlike a small town, a nation is usually much too large for direct democracy to work. No auditorium is big enough for millions of citizens to sit down together to make national laws. Instead, in a representative democracy, laws are made by a small number of officials who are elected by a vote of the people. The elected lawmakers in the United States meet in the Capitol in Washington, D.C., as the U.S. Congress. They represent the voters who elect them. As representatives of the people, they have the responsibility to decide what laws would best serve the states or districts from which they come.

Four characteristics are especially important to the U.S. system of representative democracy:

1. *Consent of the governed.* The laws passed by Congress have been approved by the people's elected representatives.

In 1992, the voters of Athens, Meigs, and Gallia counties in southern Ohio reelected Mary Abel to the Ohio House of Representatives. How is this election an example of representative democracy?

rights—the Bill of Rights. Among the rights guaranteed to every citizen are freedom of speech, freedom of the press, and freedom of religion. You will learn more about these rights in Chapter 14.

Pluses and Minuses of Representative Government Compared with monarchies and dictatorships, the U.S. system of government offers people the greatest amount of protection from harsh and unjust laws. People are doubly protected against harsh rule by the rights guaranteed in the Constitution and the power that they have as voters. Officials at all levels of government must continually earn the voters' trust. If a high official is corrupted by power, both a free press and political opponents can usually be depended on to expose his or her wrongdoing.

Strong as it is, however, representative democracy does not guarantee good and effective government. First, because many competing groups and political parties disagree about what government should do, there may be long delays before needed laws are passed. Second, a democratic system depends for its success on millions of people being interested enough in public affairs to vote intelligently. If people lose touch with their representatives or cease to care about political issues, the quality of democratic government may decline. Thomas Jefferson once wrote: "Eternal vigilance is the price of liberty." In other words, a democracy can remain healthy only so long as citizens make an effort to stay informed and to vote accordingly.

Indirectly at least, the people have given their consent to these laws because their representatives voted for them.

2. *Freedom to criticize and oppose.* Those wishing to change or do away with unwanted laws have the opportunity to express their views freely. They can criticize the president and their representatives in Congress and try to vote them out of office at the next election. Because two major political parties freely compete for votes in the United States, representatives must pay attention to the people's views. If they do not, they will probably be voted out of office.

3. *Rule by law.* The U.S. Constitution is the "supreme law of the land." It sets the boundaries, or limits, on what officials of the U.S. government can and cannot do. This "supreme law" must be obeyed by all U.S. officials, including the president. The law is a protection against abuse of power. If a president, for example, seeks to act without the approval of Congress, that action is unlawful.

4. *Guaranteed rights and liberties.* Included in the U.S. Constitution is a list of

POINTS TO REMEMBER

1 In past ages, a monarchy was the most common type of government. A single person, or monarch, exercised absolute power to make and enforce laws for the state.

2 In modern times, dictators hold power in many nations. A dictator allows the candidates of only one political party to hold office. Opposition to the dictator's government is not allowed.

3 A true democracy is a system in which the common people have the power to elect leaders and control their government.

4 The United States is an example of a representative democracy. In voting for laws, politicians represent the people who elected them to office. If politicians fail to do a good job, the voters may decide to replace them with candidates from an opposing party.

5 Every system of government has both strengths and weaknesses. A strength of representative democracy is that it enables people to protect themselves from unjust laws. A potential weakness of democracy is that people may lose interest in government and fail to carry out their responsibilities as voters.

EXERCISES

CHECKING WHAT YOU HAVE READ

For each phrase or word below, write the type of government that it describes. Write either **AB** for absolute monarchy, **DICT** for dictatorship, or **REP** for representative democracy.

_____ 1. headed by a king or queen
_____ 2. Cuba's system
_____ 3. limited by a constitution
_____ 4. consent of the governed
_____ 5. free elections involving competing parties
_____ 6. Saudi Arabia's system
_____ 7. one political party
_____ 8. power passed down from a parent to a child
_____ 9. guaranteed rights for individual citizens
_____ 10. lawmakers acting on the behalf of the voters

USING WHAT YOU HAVE READ

On a separate sheet of paper, copy the following chart. Fill in each section, or box, with as many positive and negative characteristics as you can think of.

COMPARING TYPES OF GOVERNMENT

	Representative Democracy	Absolute Monarchy	Dictatorship
Positive Characteristics			
Negative Characteristics			

THINKING ABOUT WHAT YOU HAVE READ

In a few sentences, explain how you think each type of government would respond to the following issues or problems.

1. A riot erupts in a major city. Shops are looted, and buildings are set on fire.
   a. Absolute monarchy:
   b. Dictatorship:
   c. Representative democracy:
2. A newspaper criticizes the government's leaders and policies.
   a. Absolute monarchy:
   b. Dictatorship:
   c. Representative democracy:

SKILLS: INTERPRETING POLITICAL CARTOONS

The cartoons that you might find on the editorial pages of a newspaper are called political cartoons or editorial cartoons. They are often funny. But humor is not the main purpose of these drawings. Cartoonists express their views on political issues through their cartoons. In doing so, they are trying to influence your views.

(John Trever, The Albuquerque Journal. Reprinted with special permission of North American Syndicate)

Study the cartoon above. Then answer the questions that follow. Note that the term "Banana Republic" (used in the first frame on the left) refers to any small country in the tropics whose economy is dependent upon one crop, such as bananas. In addition, the term usually means that the country's government is undemocratic and depends for support on a foreign power. People resent having their country called a "Banana Republic."

Note also that the man pictured in the cartoon is General Manuel Noriega. In 1988, when the cartoon was drawn, he was the leader of Panama. In 1989, U.S. forces invaded Panama, arrested General Noriega, and brought him to the United States to stand trial for aiding in the smuggling of illegal drugs into this country. A court found him guilty and sentenced him to a long jail term.

1. What does General Noriega mean in the first frame when he says, "This is no Banana Republic!"?   (a) He is denying that Panama is a clothing store.   (b) He is defending the reputation of his country.   (c) He is saying that Panama has no bananas.   (d) He is saying that Panama is not a republic.

2. What does the phrase "One man, one vote" usually mean?   (a) Every adult citizen is entitled to cast a vote.   (b) Only men can vote.   (c) Only one man in a country should be able to vote.   (d) Elections are usually decided by one vote.

3. In the last frame, General Noriega   (a) contradicts what he said in the first three frames   (b) thinks he is the only voter in Panama   (c) implies that democracy in other countries does not work   (d) boasts of his manly character.

4. The label "Bananama" in the last frame means that   (a) Panama has changed its name   (b) General Noriega has changed his name   (c) Panama was a banana republic in the eyes of the cartoonist   (d) the United States considered Noriega a criminal.

5. In the view of the cartoonist, Noriega's government in Panama was a/an   (a) democracy   (b) dictatorship   (c) absolute monarchy   (d) constitutional monarchy.

Federalism

LEARNING OUTCOME: Demonstrate an understanding of the concept of federalism by identifying the level of government (local, state, or national) responsible for a particular function.

A different level of government is responsible for each of the objects pictured on this page. Which object do you associate with the U.S. government in Washington, D.C.? Which object was probably created by the state government of Ohio? Which object do you think is the property of some local government such as the city government of Cleveland or Cincinnati? (Check your guesses by turning to the answers on page 73.)

You can see that the U.S. system of gov-

ernment consists of more than one government. There is the government for the nation as a whole (the government whose capital is Washington, D.C.). In addition, each of the 50 states has its own government. Finally, all across the country, there are thousands of local governments.

A political system that permits laws to be made by both a national government and separate state governments is known as a *federal system*. Other nations, such as Turkey, permit laws to be made only at one

A

B

C

67

level—the national level. The central (national) government of Turkey can give orders to the governments of Turkish cities and towns. That is not the way the system works in the United States. Here the national government in Washington does *not* give orders either to the governor of Ohio or to the mayor of Cleveland. In a federal system, a state governor and a city mayor have independent authority.

On some matters, such as controlling illegal drugs, the national government works with the state and local governments. On other matters, such as coining and printing money, the national government works alone. Which level or levels of government (local, state, or national) has the chief responsibility for dealing with particular problems? You will be learning the answers to this question in this chapter.

Federalism and the U.S. Constitution

History helps us understand why our country has a federal system. Remember that a national government did not exist before 1776. Before the Continental Congress declared independence, there were 13 separate British colonial governments (plus the British government headed by King George III). During the American Revolution, the colonies became states. Thirteen independent states, from New Hampshire to Georgia, each formed new governments. Their representatives also created a government for the new nation. But this government was weak—much weaker than the state governments.

Confederate Government   The following diagram helps us picture the relatively weak central government that existed in the early 1780s.

FROM A CONFEDERATE SYSTEM . . .

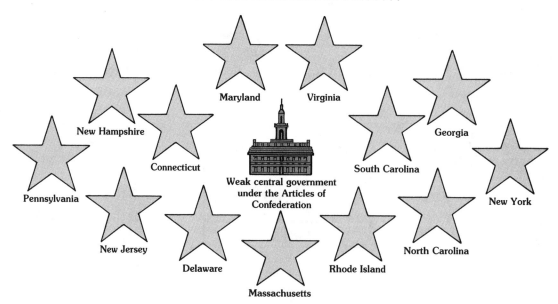

... TO A FEDERAL SYSTEM

New Hampshire   Maryland   Virginia   Georgia

Pennsylvania   Connecticut   New York   South Carolina

New Jersey   **Strong central government under the U.S. Constitution**   North Carolina

Delaware   Rhode Island

Massachusetts

The central government at this time was confederate in form. A confederacy is a group of states loosely held together by a weak central government. The document establishing a confederate plan of government for the United States was called the *Articles of Confederation.*

Plans to Strengthen Central Government   James Madison, Alexander Hamilton, and others worried about the central government under the Articles. They thought it was too weak to hold the nation together. To strengthen it, a group of leading citizens met in Philadelphia in 1787 and discussed plans for creating a new national government. The document that they wrote in Philadelphia was a new constitution for their young country. The Constitution of the United States gave the central government increased power.

The system created by the new constitution was federal in form. It gave many powers to the national government while allowing the state governments to exercise other powers.

Powers for the Nation and the States

Delegated Powers   Powers belonging to the national government are known as *delegated powers* (because they are given, or delegated, by the Constitution). The most important of these delegated powers are:

◆ the power to coin, or issue, money
◆ the power to raise an army and navy

◆ the power to tax and spend money for the general welfare

◆ the power to regulate *interstate commerce* (trade or business that crosses state lines)

◆ the power to establish post offices and post roads (highways)

♦ the power to declare war
♦ the power to conduct foreign policy
♦ the power to regulate U.S. trade with other nations.

In general, the federal government has three broad areas of responsibility. First, only the national government may deal directly with foreign governments and foreign affairs. Its power to raise an army and wage war, if necessary, is related to its prime responsibility for dealing with other countries of the world. Second, the national government is responsible for undertaking public projects that will help the nation as a whole to prosper. Running the postal system and regulating trade between the states are two examples. Third, because the U.S. Congress may tax and spend for the "general welfare," it can operate programs to help farmers, retired workers, preschool children, people with physical handicaps, and many other groups.

Reserved Powers   The U.S. Constitution does not list specific powers and responsibilities of the state governments. It does say, however, that many broad powers are *reserved* (left to) the states. The *reserved powers* belonging to Ohio and every other state include the following:

♦ power to build and maintain state roads
♦ power to provide for public education
♦ power to license motor vehicles
♦ power to regulate marriage and divorce
♦ power to oversee elections
♦ power to regulate businesses within the state (intrastate trade)
♦ power to define and punish crimes
♦ power to provide for the care of needy people
♦ power to establish public hospitals.

You can see from this list that the state government is chiefly responsible for (1) providing a wide range of public services, including education, and (2) providing for law and order by controlling crime.

Powers of Local Governments   The third level of government in the federal system—local government—is the one closest to home. The state of Ohio, like other states, is divided into small local areas known as villages, townships, school districts, cities, and counties. Each area has its own government that carries out specific functions for the people living in that area. A school district, for example, is governed by an elected board of education. Members of this board operate the public schools in the local area.

Each local government must act in accordance with state laws. The police department in Dayton must try to enforce the laws of Ohio. The high schools in Marietta must fulfill state requirements for graduation. The fire department of Akron must follow the state's guidelines for fire safety. The officials of Ashtabula County (and all other Ohio counties) must carry out the state's welfare laws and road-building programs.

Local governments can collect taxes for local needs and decide such questions as how many police officers, fire fighters, and sanitation workers to hire. In other matters, however, a local government must stay within the bounds set by state laws. It is much less independent than the other two levels of government.

A special power of local governments is the power to pass *zoning laws*. These laws divide a community's land into areas, or zones, according to their use. One zone may be used only for residences, while another is set aside for stores, and a third for industry. The construction and safety of a community's buildings are governed by local laws called building codes.

Concurrent Powers   Only the national government may operate the post office, coin money, and declare war. Only the state governments may run the public schools and issue marriage licenses and driver's licenses.

On most matters, however, all three levels of government (national, state, and local) have powers that are much alike:

◆ collect taxes
◆ operate parks

◆ build roads and highways
◆ enforce laws against crimes
◆ conduct trials in a court
◆ provide for people's welfare
◆ protect the environment
◆ set standards of public health.

Powers that are shared in common by two or more of the three levels of government are known as *concurrent powers*.

Powers That Are Forbidden

Those who created the U.S. Constitution feared that governments might become too powerful and destroy people's liberties. To prevent this, they identified certain powers that no government should have. According to the U.S. Constitution, the following powers are ones that are forbidden. *Neither* the national government *nor* the state governments may:

◆ grant *titles of nobility* (declare someone to be a duke, earl, or lord)

◆ place taxes on *exports* (U.S. goods sold abroad)

◆ punish citizens for their religious views or political opinions

◆ keep someone in prison without a trial.

POINTS TO REMEMBER

1 Federalism is a system that gives some powers to a national government and other powers to state governments.

2 Every citizen of Ohio is subject to the laws of three levels of government (the national government, the Ohio government, and several local governments).

3 Foreign policy and military defense are the special concern of the federal, or U.S., government.

4 Education, welfare, and law and order are among the most important functions of state and local governments.

5 Local governments include counties and school districts as well as cities, villages, and townships. Each local government must carry out state laws.

6 Many powers such as taxation and law enforcement belong to all three levels of government.

EXERCISES

CHECKING WHAT YOU HAVE READ

Choose the letter of the phrase that best completes each statement or answers each question.

1. Printing money is the responsibility of (a) the Ohio government (b) the U.S. government (c) both the national and state governments (d) your local government.
2. Federalism means that (a) all power belongs to the national government (b) a state government has very little power (c) a national government has less power than the state governments (d) laws are made by three levels of government.
3. Mail delivery is a function of which level of government? (a) national (b) state (c) local (d) both state and local
4. Which power belongs *only* to the U.S. government? (a) the power to collect taxes (b) the power to make treaties with foreign governments (c) the power to punish crimes (d) the power to conduct trials in court
5. Supervising elections is a function of which level of government? (a) national (b) state (c) local (d) all of the above
6. Enforcement of building codes is a function of which level of government? (a) national (b) state (c) local (d) all of the above
7. Trade between Springfield, Ohio, and Chicago, Illinois, is an example of (a) interstate trade (b) intrastate trade (c) international trade (d) delegated powers.
8. Placing a heavy tax on exports to Japan would be a power exercised by (a) the government of the United States (b) the government of Ohio (c) the government of Cleveland (d) none of the above.
9. Concurrent powers are those exercised by (a) only the national government (b) only the state governments (c) both the national government and state governments (d) two city governments.
10. Powers belonging to the national government are (a) delegated by the U.S. Constitution (b) forbidden to the states (c) unlimited (d) subject to the laws of Ohio.

USING WHAT YOU HAVE READ

Imagine that you are seeking government help in dealing with various problems. For each problem, indicate the level of government to which you would go for assistance. Write **NATIONAL, STATE,** or **LOCAL.**

1. You have a complaint about Japan's methods for selling its cars in the United States.
2. You think a traffic light should be installed at a busy city intersection.
3. You want to know the requirements for being licensed to drive a motor vehicle.
4. As a coin collector, you need information about the number of pennies and nickels minted in 1927.

72

5. You want to know what parks and other recreational facilities are available in southern Ohio.
6. You need assistance in rescuing a cat from the top branch of a tree.

THINKING ABOUT WHAT YOU HAVE READ

1. Which level of government do you think has the greatest effect on your daily life? Use examples to explain your answer.
2. Draw a cartoon that shows the relationship between the U.S. government and Ohio's government.

SKILLS: CREATING A CHART

On a separate sheet of paper, copy the chart below. Complete the chart by placing an X under the level of government that exercises each of the listed powers. Remember that more than one level of government can exercise a power. If no level of government can exercise a power, write NONE in all three spaces. To help you get started, the first line of the chart has been completed.

GOVERNMENT POWERS

	Federal Power	State Power	Local Power
1. Coining money	X		
2. Granting titles of nobility			
3. Conducting foreign policy			
4. Putting out city fires			
5. Collecting taxes			
6. Regulating foreign trade			
7. Regulating interstate trade			
8. Conducting elections			
9. Enforcing laws			
10. Passing laws that disagree with the U.S. Constitution			

Answers to picture quiz on page 67: **A.** The coin is minted by the national, or U.S., government; **B.** The license plate is issued by the state government of Ohio; **C.** The parking meter belongs to a local government.

10

Three Branches of Government

LEARNING OUTCOME: Identify the main function of each branch of government (executive, legislative, judicial) at the national, state, and local levels.

Imagine that it is New Year's Day, the first day of the year 2001. You are watching a football game on television when suddenly, in the middle of the second half, the image on the screen switches to the president's office in the White House. A grim-looking president announces:

My fellow Americans: You are aware of the war that has spread from northern Africa to the Middle East and southern Asia. This war places the peace of the world and the security of our nation in dire peril. As your president, I am taking emergency action to meet this crisis. First of all, I hereby declare that I will soon double the size of the U.S. armed forces by calling one million young men and women into service. Second, to pay for emergency war measures, I must inform all U.S. taxpayers that they must pay an emergency tax of 500 dollars no later than the end of this month. Failure to pay the tax on time will result in a one-

year prison sentence without trial. I call upon all patriotic Americans to make the sacrifices needed to meet this terrible threat from abroad.

Fortunately, this speech is imaginary. The U.S. Constitution does *not* give the president the power to act like a dictator. Instead, the Constitution provides for *separation of powers*. It divides the U.S. government into three major parts, or branches. The president is the leader of just one of these branches—the executive branch. Two other branches, the legislative branch and the judicial branch, have independent powers of their own. The chief reason for their being independent is to prevent any one official, like the president, from having too much power.

In his speech, the imaginary president failed to mention Congress. But according to the Constitution, only Congress, as the legislative branch, has the power to raise taxes. A president therefore cannot tell people that they must pay an emergency tax if Congress has not voted for that tax.

74

You will learn in this chapter about the importance of separation of powers among the three branches of government. You will see how the idea of separation of powers applies not only to the national government but also to the state and local governments.

Legislative, Executive, and Judicial Powers

All governments have three kinds of power. There is *legislative power,* which is the power to make laws. There is *executive power,* which is the power to enforce, or carry out, the laws. Finally, there is *judicial power,* which is the power to interpret the laws in a courtroom and to judge whether or not a citizen has obeyed the laws.

In the United States, *every* government recognizes the principle of separation of powers. In other words, it gives the three types of powers to three separate and independent branches. The diagram below illustrates this concept.

SEPARATION OF POWERS

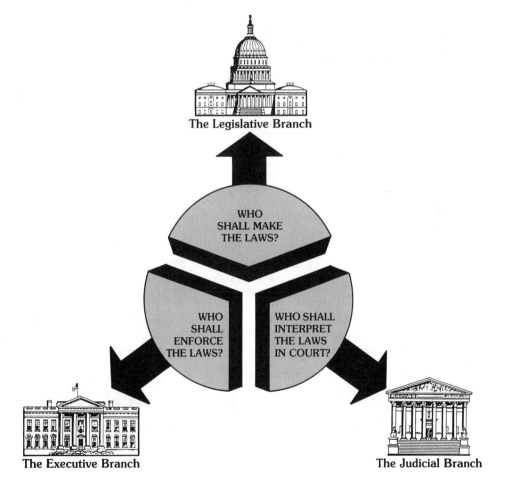

The Legislative Branch

WHO SHALL MAKE THE LAWS?

WHO SHALL ENFORCE THE LAWS?

WHO SHALL INTERPRET THE LAWS IN COURT?

The Executive Branch

The Judicial Branch

The Legislative Branch

The U.S. Constitution says that a two-house *Congress* shall have the legislative power to make laws for the nation. Congress has the power, for example, to make laws concerning taxes, the post office, the armed forces, the issuing of money, and the regulation of *commerce* (trade or business) between the states. The officials elected to make the laws come from all 50 states. Each state, regardless of its size, sends just two elected lawmakers, known as senators, to the smaller house of Congress—the *U.S. Senate.* Each state also sends another group of lawmakers, known as representatives, to the larger house of Congress, the *U.S. House of Representatives.* Because Ohio has a large population, it can send many more representatives to the House than Vermont, Rhode Island, or other states with small populations.

The legislative branch that makes laws for the state of Ohio meets in the state capitol in Columbus. It is called the Ohio *General Assembly.* The General Assembly's powers to make Ohio's law derive from this clause in Ohio's constitution:

> The legislative power of the state shall be vested in a General Assembly consisting of a senate and house of representatives . . . .

Like the Congress of the United States, the General Assembly of Ohio is made up of two separate houses, or groups. Meeting in the smaller house—the Ohio *Senate*—are 33 elected senators, who represent various districts around the state. Meeting in the larger house—the Ohio *House of Representatives*—are 99 representatives, who come from smaller districts around the state. The laws made by the General Assembly cover a huge number of subjects:

Both the U.S. Capitol (above) and Ohio's Capitol (below) consist of two legislative bodies: a house of representatives, which meets in one wing, and a senate, which meets in the other wing. (*Library of Congress; Ohio Historical Society*)

schools, roads, bridges, crimes, taxes, business, agriculture, forests, lakes, rivers, pollution, prisons, housing, health, land use, wildlife, marriage, and divorce—almost everything under the sun.

At the local level, most of Ohio's cities have given legislative power to a group called the *city council.* Unlike the Congress and the General Assembly, a city council meets as a single body, not as two houses. Council members are elected by the city's voters either "at large" (representing the entire city) or as representatives of specific districts, or neighborhoods. The lawmaking power of the city council is not as great as that of the General Assembly. Nevertheless, within limits set by the state constitution, a city council can legislate (make laws) on a wide range of local problems, including garbage collection, police protection, traffic management, and parking regulations.

The Executive Branch

Who has the responsibility for seeing that the laws enacted by the legislative branch are fully carried out? You already know the answer: the *executive branch.*

At all levels of government, the executive branch employs the largest number of people. At the national level, for example, thousands of workers in the Defense Department and State Department carry out laws and programs dealing with foreign affairs. Thousands of others carry out laws concerning the national parks, Indian reservations, air and water pollution, railroad safety, airplane safety, and so on. (You will learn more about these workers in the executive branch in Chapter 13).

Each level of government (national, state, and local) has a different official in charge of its executive branch.

◆ In the U.S. government, the chief executive is the president.
◆ In state government, the official who directs Ohio's executive branch is the governor.
◆ In local government, the official responsible for the work of various city departments (police, fire, sanitation, and so on) may be either a *mayor* or a *city manager.* A mayor is an official elected to his or her office by direct vote of city residents. A city manager is appointed, or hired, by the city's legislative body—the city council. Many cities, including Cleveland and Columbus, have mayors, who are directly responsible to the voters. Other cities, including Dayton and Cincinnati, prefer to hire a city manager, who brings to the job expert knowledge on dealing with city problems.

TEST YOURSELF

The following questions refer to information presented on pages 74–77.

1. Why does the U.S. Constitution provide for separation of powers?

2. At the national level, what is the name of (*a*) the legislative branch and (*b*) the official at the head of the executive branch?

3. At the state level in Ohio, what is the name of (*a*) the legislative branch and (*b*) the official in charge of the executive branch?

4. In city government, what is the name of (*a*) the legislative branch, (*b*) an elected chief executive in some cities, and (*c*) an appointed chief executive in other cities?

The Judicial Branch

The third branch of government is the *judicial branch,* which consists of hundreds of courts. The judges who work for this branch conduct trials and interpret the laws in specific cases. There is one court system at the national level and a separate court system in each state.

Federal Courts The U.S. government is often referred to as the federal government. The courts in its judicial branch are known as federal courts. The federal judges who preside over these courts hear cases involving the laws of Congress (*not* the laws of a state legislature).

For example, a federal judge may hear a criminal case involving charges that one Joe Dokes printed counterfeit money in his basement. A judge in another federal court may hear a civil (noncriminal) case. We can imagine a case, for example, in which one Gloria Garcia complains that she has been cheated out of Social Security benefits. Since there are federal laws concerning both counterfeiting and Social Security, federal judges (not state judges) hear such cases.

The U.S. judicial branch is organized into three kinds of courts. There are (1) a large number of *district courts,* (2) several *courts of appeals,* and (3) one *supreme court.* What are the responsibilities of each kind of court?

The United States is divided into over 90 areas, or districts. Each district has its own federal court, or district court. Ohio, for example, has two district courts. One court in Cleveland serves the northern half of the state. A second court in Columbus serves the southern half. The main function of every district court is to hold trials arising under federal laws. If Joe Dokes were arrested in Cleveland, the federal district

The U.S. Supreme Court hears cases in this grand building in Washington, D.C. (*Collection of the Supreme Court of the United States*)

court in that city would conduct his trial. If Gloria Garcia lived in Cincinnati, her lawyer would argue her case in the federal court in Columbus.

Now suppose that the *jury* at Joe Dokes's trial finds him guilty of counterfeiting. (A jury is a group of citizens who, in a criminal case, decide whether the accused person is or is not guilty.) Dokes's lawyer may want a "higher" (more powerful) court to review the decision of the district court to see whether it was just. The lawyer knows that 12 courts in the U.S. judicial branch have the responsibility of reviewing cases originally tried in the district courts. (These higher courts are known as courts of appeals.) Dokes's lawyer would appeal the cases to a group of federal judges serving Ohio and three other states (Kentucky, Michigan, and Tennessee).

No trials are held in a court of appeals. Instead, a panel of three or more judges rules on whether or not the district court's understanding of the law was proper and fair in the case at issue. The court of appeals can either agree or disagree with the lower court's decision. If it disagrees, the lower court's decision is reversed, or overturned. Otherwise, the original decision stands (remains as it was).

At the highest level of the federal court system is the U.S. Supreme Court. It is the court of last resort, meaning that it has the last word in all cases brought before it. Its decisions are final and cannot be appealed further. Nine justices sit on the U.S. Supreme Court. They decide each case by majority vote.

State and Local Courts   The judicial branch of Ohio's government is organized like that of the U.S. government's. It has (1) lower courts that conduct trials, (2) courts of appeals that may review the lower courts' decisions, and (3) a supreme court that may review the appeals courts' decisions. The cases heard in Ohio courts deal only with the state laws enacted by the Ohio General Assembly.

Each of Ohio's 88 counties is served by a *court of common pleas*. This is the trial court, or lower court, in Ohio's judicial system. Some of the cases tried in a court of common pleas are criminal cases dealing with serious crimes (murder and theft, for example). Others are civil cases—lawsuits between citizens (divorce cases, accidental damages to property, the breaking of contracts, and other cases).

Ohio also has *courts of appeals*, which hear appeals from the lower (county) courts. The state is divided into 12 appellate (or appeals) districts. Each district has one court of appeals.

Final appeals are heard by Ohio's most powerful court, the Ohio *Supreme Court*. In reviewing cases from the state courts of appeals, the Supreme Court interprets the Ohio Constitution. In each case, the seven judges on the state Supreme Court decide whether a state law has been correctly interpreted by the lower courts.

On the local level, towns and cities have municipal courts. These courts enforce local laws, such as ones concerning parking violations, speeding tickets, and disturbing the peace.

Does the court system seem complicated? Studying the diagram on page 81 will help you to understand it better. Notice that the U.S. Supreme Court stands at the top of both the federal court system and the state system. Even Ohio's highest court can be overruled by the highest court of all—the Supreme Court of the United States.

POINTS TO REMEMBER

1 Separation of powers means that the powers of government are held by separate branches of government. A legislative branch has the power to make laws. An executive branch has the power to enforce the laws. A judicial branch has the power to interpret laws in a courtroom.

2 At the national level, Congress is the legislative branch, the president heads the executive branch, and the U.S. Supreme Court and other federal courts make up the judicial branch.

3 At the state level, the General Assembly is the legislative branch, the governor heads the executive branch, and the Ohio Supreme Court and other state courts make up the judicial branch.

4 In Ohio's cities, local laws are made by a city council (the legislative branch) and carried out by either an elected mayor or appointed city manager (heading the executive branch).

5 County courts—the courts of common pleas—are the trial courts in Ohio's judicial branch.

EXERCISES

CHECKING WHAT YOU HAVE READ

For each phrase (1–10), write whether it describes (A) the legislative branch, (B) the executive branch, or (C) the judicial branch. Answer by letter: A, B, or C.

_____   1. headed by the president at the national level

_____   2. holds trials

_____   3. has power to make laws

_____   4. has the largest number of government workers

_____   5. consists of lower courts and appeals courts

_____   6. interprets the laws

_____   7. headed by a mayor at the local level

_____   8. consists of senators and representatives

_____   9. carries out laws and programs voted by Congress

_____   10. carries out laws and programs voted by the General Assembly

USING WHAT YOU HAVE READ

On a separate sheet of paper, copy the following chart:

BRANCHES OF GOVERNMENT

	National (Federal) Government	State Government	Local Government
Legislative Branch			
Executive Branch			
Judicial Branch			

Complete the chart by entering the names of the following officials and government bodies: MAYOR, CONGRESS, GENERAL ASSEMBLY, CITY MANAGER, PRESIDENT, U.S. SUPREME COURT, COURTS OF COMMON PLEAS, OHIO SUPREME COURT, GOVERNOR, MUNICIPAL COURTS, U.S. COURTS OF APPEALS, CITY COUNCIL.

THINKING ABOUT WHAT YOU HAVE READ

1. Imagine a local government that gives all legislative, executive, and judicial powers to just one person. Write a paragraph describing how such a government might operate.
2. Reread the speech by an imaginary president on page 74. Explain how the actions threatened in the speech would violate the idea of separation of powers.

SKILLS: INTERPRETING DIAGRAMS

The court system is complicated. Only certain cases may be heard by state courts, while other cases are heard by the federal (national) courts. Which cases may be tried and appealed by which type of court? A diagram like the one that follows helps us to see at a glance how both Ohio's system and the federal system are organized. Arrows in the diagram show the route taken by different cases as they go from a trial court to an appeals court.

Following the arrows, read the descriptions for each type of court. Then answer the questions on page 82.

FEDERAL AND STATE COURTS

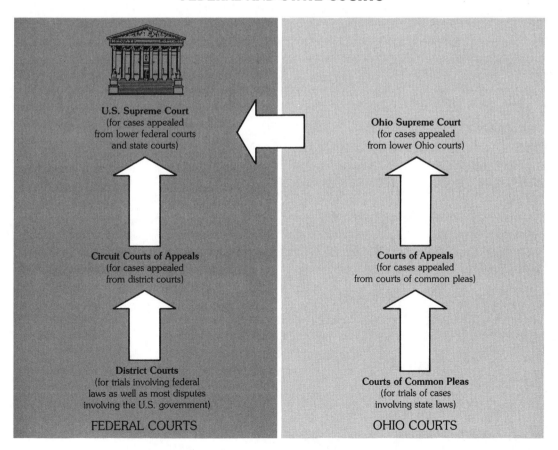

U.S. Supreme Court
(for cases appealed from lower federal courts and state courts)

Ohio Supreme Court
(for cases appealed from lower Ohio courts)

Circuit Courts of Appeals
(for cases appealed from district courts)

Courts of Appeals
(for cases appealed from courts of common pleas)

District Courts
(for trials involving federal laws as well as most disputes involving the U.S. government)

Courts of Common Pleas
(for trials of cases involving state laws)

FEDERAL COURTS   OHIO COURTS

1. Which branch of the federal government is included in this diagram?
2. Which branch of Ohio's government is included in this diagram?
3. What is unique about the powers of the U.S. Supreme Court?
4. If someone robbed a U.S. post office: (a) In which type of court would the case be tried?   (b) In which type of court might the case be heard on appeal?
5. If someone were accused of breaking a criminal law of Ohio: (a) In which type of court would the case be tried?   (b) In which type of court might the case be heard on appeal?
6. Is it accurate to say that no case that originates in an Ohio court can go beyond the Ohio Supreme Court? Explain your answer.

11

The Lawmaking Process

LEARNING OUTCOME: Describe the process for making, amending, or removing laws.

Newspapers and TV news programs are filled with reports about public problems like these:

◆ congested roads and highways
◆ illegal drugs
◆ violent crimes
◆ not enough job opportunities for teen-agers
◆ unsafe working conditions
◆ polluted rivers and lakes
◆ discrimination against women and minorities
◆ rising costs of health care
◆ child abuse.

State laws and federal laws already exist to deal with these problems. Even so, the problems continue. Perhaps a citizen or an elected lawmaker can think of a way to improve the laws so that government can act more effectively to solve particular problems.

Suppose, for example, that you have an idea for dealing with the problem of child abuse. You describe your proposed law in a letter, which you send to your representative in the U.S. House of Representatives. We shall call her "Joan Sloan." After a few days, you receive a reply from Representative Sloan. She expresses enthusiasm for your idea and announces that she intends to act on it. What steps would Representative Sloan have to take to turn your idea for a law into an actual law?

This chapter will describe the process for making laws at both the state and national levels. After reading it, you will understand what happens when a citizen like you or a legislator like Representative Sloan has an idea for changing the law.

Steps for Enacting a Law

The lawmaking process consists of a number of steps. The sequence of steps is about the same in both the state legislature (Ohio's General Assembly) and the national legislature (the U.S. Congress).

Follow steps one through ten.

83

Step One: Introducing a Bill First, your idea for a law would have to be drafted, or written, in the form of a *bill*. A bill is a formal proposal for a law. Anyone can draft a bill (although it is usually done by someone with legal training). The process for considering a bill begins when a member of the legislature introduces the bill. Representative Sloan, for example, would physically carry her bill on child abuse onto the floor of the U.S. House of Representatives and drop it into a wooden box known as the hopper. The bill is given a number. The Child Abuse Bill, for example, might be numbered HR-123.

Bills may be introduced in *either* of the legislature's two houses. (One exception: on the federal level, tax bills must originate in the House of Representatives.) Remember that two groups of lawmakers—or houses—meet separately to consider proposed laws. Ohio's government and the U.S. government call their two houses by the same names. Both have a House of Representatives (the larger house) and a Senate (the smaller house). In a typical week, hundreds of bills on dozens of subjects are introduced in both the state and national legislatures.

Step Two: Considering a Bill in Committee After being introduced in the U.S. House of Representatives, our bill HR-123 goes to an appropriate *committee*. A committee is a small group of legislators who study bills on a particular subject. Each house has committees that specialize in education, labor, health, welfare, taxes, agriculture, and other subjects. The Judiciary Committee in the U.S. House of Representatives deals with bills that define crimes. This committee would probably be the one to study a bill on child abuse.

Most bills never go further than the committees that first look at them. They may quickly be filed away and forgotten. Or a committee may listen to arguments for and against a certain bill and then vote against the bill. Of course, there are some bills that receive the approval of a majority of committee members. Only these bills make it to the next step in the lawmaking process. Let us assume that HR-123 is among them.

Step Three: Vote on the House Floor If a committee approves a bill, it is returned to the full house (the chamber where all lawmakers meet to conduct official business). Here all members of the House of Representatives have an opportunity to debate and vote on the bill. Speakers in favor of the bill explain how it would help to solve a public problem. Those opposing the bill point out its weaknesses and the possible harm it could do if enacted into law. A vote is then taken.

Let us assume that a sizable majority of the House of Representatives vote in favor of HR-123.

Steps Four, Five, and Six: Action by the Other House A bill enacted by one house must then go through identical steps in the other house. The bill is introduced in the other house (step four) and assigned to a committee. The committee may ignore, reject, or approve the bill (step five). If approved by committee, the bill is debated and voted on by the full house (step six).

In the case of HR-123, a Senate committee approves the bill and a majority of senators vote for the bill on the Senate floor. But the bill enacted by the Senate differs in several respects from the bill enacted by the House.

Step Seven: Referral to a Conference Committee If the two houses pass different versions of a bill, a few members of both houses confer on how to overcome their differences. They meet in a special two-house committee known as a

THE PATH OF LEGISLATION (HOW A BILL BECOMES A LAW)

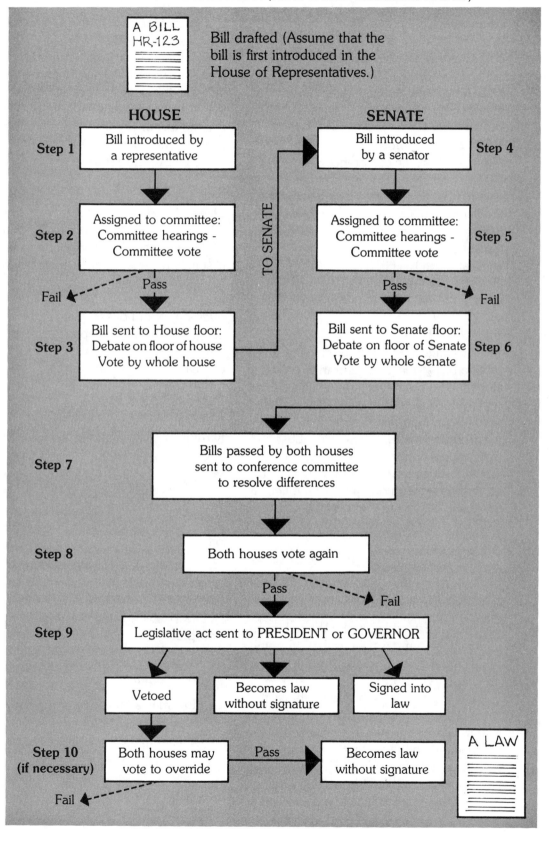

conference committee. Committee members debate the pros and cons of the House bill and the Senate bill. By changing a word here and a phrase there, they may succeed in creating a compromise bill that is acceptable to both houses.

Step Eight: Another Vote by Both Houses Now the conference committee's bill must be approved by both the House and the Senate. The House votes again; the Senate votes again. Usually there is little debate at this stage, and the bill passes both houses.

What started as HR-123 is now an Act of Congress, called the Child Abuse Act. Even so, it is not yet the law of the land.

Step Nine: Decision by the Chief Executive Having finished its lawmaking work on one bill, the legislative branch passes it along to the chief executive for his or her approval. As you know, the nation's chief executive is the president.

Let us assume that the Child Abuse Act (formerly HR-123) has the president's approval. The president would then write his or her signature on one page of the act. At this point, the act of Congress would officially become a new law of the United States.

What happens if the president dislikes parts of an act but decides to allow it to become law anyway? In that case, the president would not do anything with the act. The measure would sit in the White House unsigned for ten days. After that time, the act becomes law automatically without the president's signature.

What happens if the president thinks the act of Congress is unwise and wants to stop it from becoming law? In that case, he or she would *veto* the act by (1) not signing it and (2) sending it back to Congress. The word veto is Latin for "I forbid." The vetoed measure is usually accompanied by a

written statement from the president giving reasons for the veto.

At the state level, a bill enacted by Ohio's General Assembly goes to the governor, who has the same choices as the president. The governor may decide to (1) sign the act into law *or* (2) allow the act to become law without signing it *or* (3) veto the act by sending it back to the General Assembly.

Step Ten (If Necessary): Attempt to Override A veto does not necessarily put an end to lawmakers' hopes for their bill. They can either (1) change the bill so that it stands a better chance of satisfying the president (or governor) or (2) try to *override,* or get around, the veto. In order to override, both houses vote on the original bill (as enacted in step eight) one more time. This time, if they wish their bill to become law without the president's signature, more than a majority of the lawmakers must vote for it. Congress can override a president's veto only if a bill receives at least two-thirds of the votes in each house.

On the state level, Ohio's General Assembly can override a governor's veto only if a bill receives at least three-fifths of the votes in each house. Because of the many votes needed, an override does not happen often.

TEST YOURSELF

The following questions refer to information presented on pages 83–86.

1. Define the following terms: *bill, conference committee, veto, override.*

2. How may a bill be introduced in Ohio's Senate? (Assume that the process is the same as that for introducing a bill in one of the houses of Congress.)

3. List four ways in which a bill like HR-123 could be defeated.

Where Bills Come From

In this chapter, we have imagined that the idea for HR-123 came from an average citizen—you. Of the thousands of bills considered by Congress and state legislatures every year, a small percentage do in fact originate with average citizens. Most, however, come from other sources.

A Legislator's Proposals Legislators in both houses of Congress and Ohio's General Assembly introduce bills on subjects of vital interest to the people they serve. The job of drafting a bill on a particular subject is usually assigned to someone on the senator's or representative's staff.

A Pressure Group's Proposals *Pressure groups* also draft a number of bills on subjects that concern them. A pressure group is an organization that has a special interest in laws that directly affect their group. For example, business groups want laws that reduce their taxes. Labor unions want laws that protect the interests of union members. Besides drafting bills, pressure groups hire *lobbyists*—people who specialize in talking with legislators. Lobbyists try to influence lawmakers to vote for bills that serve the interests of a particular group.

A President's or Governor's Proposals As the nation's chief leader, the president often suggests bills to Congress. Sometimes members of the president's staff actually write bills on many subjects. They give these bills to selected representatives or senators to introduce in one house or the other. Presidential support or opposition can greatly influence the success of a bill before Congress.

Similarly, Ohio's governor directs members of his or her staff to write bills to be introduced in the General Assembly.

Citizens' Proposals In Ohio, some bills do not even go to the General Assembly. Instead, by a procedure called the *initiative*, a citizen or a pressure group may submit a proposed law directly to the voters. First, copies of the proposed law or bill are circulated to thousands of citizens. A certain number of them must sign their names to a petition asking that the bill be placed on the ballot. If enough signatures are collected, the proposed law is put on a statewide ballot. Voters have a choice of voting either "yes" (approve) or "no" (disapprove). If a majority vote yes, the proposal becomes law.

Changing and Removing Laws

No matter how they are drafted and adopted, laws are not always successful or popular. Some laws do not accomplish what they are intended to do. There may be weaknesses in the way a particular law is worded. The executive branch may fail to enforce the law in the way the legislature intended. Sometimes a newly elected group of legislators may disagree with a law and wish to change it. Finally, as time passes, conditions change, and the original need for an old law may disappear.

An unwanted law can be either changed or removed altogether in four different ways.

88 THE OHIO CITIZEN

1. Legislative Action The legislature may pass a new law that either changes or *repeals* (removes) an existing law. To do this, Congress or the state legislature must introduce a bill, consider it in committee, and go through all the other steps in the lawmaking process.

2. Voter Action In Ohio, voters can abolish laws through a process known as the *referendum*. Petitions are circulated among qualified Ohio voters. If a certain number of voters sign the petitions, a question is printed on a statewide ballot. In effect, the question asks: Should Law X be eliminated, or repealed? If a majority vote "yes," the law in question ceases to be a law.

Like the initiative process, the referendum process takes much effort and time. Neither process occurs very often.

3. Court Action Yet another way that laws are changed is through *judicial review* (or review by a court). You may remember that the chief function of the judicial branch of government is to decide how the laws shall be interpreted in specific cases. The U.S. Supreme Court performs this function in reviewing both state laws and federal laws. Using its power of judicial review, this court decides whether a certain law agrees with the principles of the U.S. Constitution. The court may rule that the law does not agree with the Constitution. If this happens, the law is *unconstitutional*. Such a law is no longer valid. In effect, it ceases to exist.

Ohio's courts also have the power to review state laws (but not federal laws). If a state law does not conform to Ohio's state constitution, a state court may void the law by declaring it unconstitutional.

4. Constitutional Change The most difficult method for changing laws is to attempt to change the most important law of all—the constitution. Both the U.S. Constitution and Ohio's state constitution can have new clauses added to them. Such added clauses are known as amendments. The most common method for amending the U.S. Constitution involves two steps. First, the two houses of Congress pass by a two-thirds vote a proposal for an amendment. Next, copies of the proposed amendment go to the different state legislatures. If three-fourths of the states vote to ratify the amendment, it is added to the Constitution.

The writers of the U.S. and Ohio constitutions wanted the processes for amending a constitution to be difficult. They wanted to make sure that constitutions would be changed only for serious reasons.

POINTS TO REMEMBER

1 The state legislature and the U.S. Congress follow similar procedures for making laws.

2 A bill is introduced in either of the two houses of a legislature. It must be passed by a majority vote of both houses before it can become a law.

3 Committees consider bills but stop most of them from being considered by the rest of the legislature.

4 Each house may change a bill as it passes through the steps of the lawmaking process. That is why bills passed by both houses must often be referred to a conference committee to resolve differences in the two versions.

5 After both houses have passed an identically worded version of a bill, it is sent to the president for his or her signature. If the president signs the act of Congress, it becomes law automatically. If the president vetoes an act by not signing it, the document returns to the two houses of Congress.

6 Congress can override a president's veto if it passes the bill again by a two-thirds vote in each house.

7 A law can be amended or removed in several ways. The legislature can do this by passing a bill. The voters can do this by referendum (an election on an issue). A court can declare a law null and void if it finds the law to be unconstitutional. Finally, Congress can propose a constitutional amendment and submit it to the states for ratification.

EXERCISES

CHECKING WHAT YOU HAVE READ

Assume that a certain bill is introduced in the Ohio Senate. The steps for turning this bill into a state law are listed below, but out of order. On a separate piece of paper, renumber the steps in the correct order.

1. _____ The bill is debated and voted upon by the Ohio House of Representatives.
2. _____ The bill is introduced in the Ohio Senate.
3. _____ After passing the Senate, the bill is introduced in the House.
4. _____ The bill is sent to a conference committee.
5. _____ After enactment by both houses, the bill is sent to the governor.
6. _____ The bill is studied by a House committee.
7. _____ The bill is debated and voted on by the Senate.
8. _____ The governor vetoes the bill.
9. _____ The Ohio General Assembly overrides the veto.
10. _____ The bill is studied by a Senate committee.

USING WHAT YOU HAVE READ

Imagine that you live in Washington, D.C., as one of Ohio's lawmakers in the U.S. House of Representatives. Explain what you would do in each situation described below.

1. A bill on air pollution comes to your committee. You believe the bill would weaken the nation's laws on air pollution. What could you do to see that this bill is defeated?
2. You believe the tax laws should be changed to give a special tax break to parents who pay for a child's college education. What could you do to carry out your idea for changing the law?
3. You worked hard for a bill that was passed by Congress but then vetoed by the president. What could you do to keep hopes for your bill alive?

THINKING ABOUT WHAT YOU HAVE READ

1. Assume that your class wants to change an Ohio law by the process of initiative. What are the basic steps in this process?
2. Think of some public problem that might be remedied by passing a new law. (Refer to the list of problems on page 83.) As a class, (a) choose one problem, (b) propose a solution to the problem that involves government action, and (c) write a petition of initiative.

    Circulate the petition among the students in your school and perhaps among their parents or guardians as well. Discuss the results of your petition drive. What reasons did people give in support of or opposition to your petition? How difficult would it be to put an initiative measure on the ballot? (*Note:* For an initiative measure to be placed on the ballot, Ohio requires the following: [1] The total number of signatures on the petitions must equal at least 10 percent of the number of people who voted for governor in the last election. [2] The signatures must have been obtained from at least 44 of the state's 88 counties.)

SKILLS: INTERPRETING FLOWCHARTS

Flowcharts are often seen in newspapers and magazines. The purpose of a flowchart is to take a complicated subject and present it in a simple, usable manner. Flowcharts are especially useful in describing the steps of a process and the movement from one step to the next.

Carefully study the chart on page 85. Then, answer the questions.

1. What is the difference in meaning between the solid arrows in the flowchart and the broken arrows?
2. What happens to those bills that fail to receive a favorable vote at either step 2 or step 5?
3. Why is it often necessary for bills to go through step 7?
4. What are two ways that a bill can become law without a president's or governor's signature?
5. Why is it more difficult for Congress to pass a vetoed bill at step 10 than to pass that bill originally at step 8?
6. Why is step 10 labeled "if necessary"?
7. How would the flowchart change to show the process if a bill is introduced in the Senate? In other words, if you were to redraw the chart, how would you change the positions of the first six steps?

12

The Role of Political Parties

LEARNING OUTCOME: Understand that the major role of political parties in a democracy is to provide a choice in governmental leadership.

Think of a school election for president and treasurer of the student body. James K. decides to run for president entirely by himself without anyone to help him. Two other candidates, Valerie G. and Lisa M., take a different approach. They decide to support each other and call upon a large number of friends to help them with their campaign. Valerie, as a candidate for president, urges everyone to vote for Lisa for treasurer. Lisa in turn urges her friends to vote for Valerie for president. In effect, the group of friends supporting Valerie and Lisa for election as class officers are an example of a political party.

A *political party* is an organization whose chief purpose is to elect members of the party to office. Most members of the party have similar ideas about government policy. If the party's candidates succeed in winning election, they have the opportunity to run the government according to their ideas of what should be done.

This chapter explains the role played by political parties in the United States and in Ohio. It asks you to imagine yourself as a candidate running for the top job in Ohio's government. What part would political parties play in your effort to become the next governor of Ohio?

Nominating Candidates: The Spring Primaries

Since the mid-1800s, the Democratic party and the Republican party have competed for votes as the two major political parties in the United States. Membership in each party is open to *every* American citizen. Simply by saying "I'm a Democrat" or "I'm a Republican" qualifies you for being accepted into the party of your choice. If

91

you are a loyal party member, you will vote regularly for the party's candidates at election time. You might also donate money to the party to help pay for the campaigns of its candidates.

Campaigning for Governor The most active members of a party are the politicians who want to hold government offices. Suppose that you are a Republican politician in Ohio. You have just celebrated your 30th birthday. Imagine further that you have ambitions to be elected governor of the state. How would you go about the difficult task of winning election to this high office?

First, you need to be selected, or *nominated,* by the Republican voters of Ohio in a spring election known as a *primary.* In preparation for the primary, you have already announced that you are a candidate for the Republican nomination for governor. For weeks, you have been traveling all across the state to shake voters' hands, make speeches, and appear in interviews and ads on television. You plan to debate the other candidates who have also entered the Republican primary race. Only one Republican can be that party's nominee. At this point, you are not worrying too much about the Democratic candidates for governor. In the spring, your main focus is to beat rivals in your own party.

Ohio holds its primary elections on a Tuesday in May. On that day, the Republicans hold one election for their party, while the Democrats hold a separate election. As one of the Republican candidates for governor, your name will appear only on the Republican ballot. Only voters who call themselves Republicans will be permitted to enter the voting booth that presents the Republican ballot. (At the same time, Democratic voters will be allowed to vote only for Democratic candidates.)

The Nominees of Two Major Parties The primary ballots are counted. On the evening news, you learn that you have won the Republican nomination. You are now the one and only Republican candidate for governor. Your Republican rivals call to congratulate you and offer their support in the coming months. You will need their help and the help of the entire party. After all, you now must face and defeat the winner of the Democratic primary. Let us call your Democratic opponent "Sam Sandusky."

Before plunging into the fall campaign, notice how the two parties have simplified voters' choices in November. Before the May primaries, seven candidates (four Republicans and three Democrats) were running for governor. Now the choice is down to just two major candidates—you as the Republican nominee and Sam Sandusky as the Democratic nominee.

Campaign and General Election

After the primaries comes the next stage of your long campaign to become governor. You are now looking ahead to the date of the *general election* in November. An opinion poll in June shows that 52 percent of Ohio's voters would vote for Sandusky if they could vote today. But of course, you have plenty of time to overtake and defeat your Democratic rival. Whether you win or lose will depend in part on how much support you receive from members of your own party.

Party Support   How can the party help you? First, those who identify themselves as Republicans will most probably vote for you in November. Second, many Republicans will campaign for you. The party has committees in every county in the state. Each committee has hundreds of volunteer workers to help with Republican campaigns. They mail campaign literature for party nominees to the voters. They arrange for campaign rallies in the local area. (A rally is like a large pep assembly, complete with banners, bands, and balloons.) Finally, the party helps to raise funds to pay for campaigns. Buying television time for your campaign ads costs hundreds of thousands of dollars. You can raise only a small part of the money yourself. Much of the rest will have to be donated by party members who want to see you elected.

National Party Conventions

While you are campaigning for governor of Ohio, other Republicans and Democrats are campaigning for other offices in Ohio and across the nation. On the national level, the campaign that receives the most attention is the one for U.S. president. Early in the year, candidates of the same party compete to win their party's nomination for president. They do so by entering primary races in Ohio and many other states. Voters in the primaries choose *delegates* from each state to attend a national convention of the party. In July or August, the delegates assemble in a huge auditorium to perform three main tasks: (1) nominate the party's candidate for president, (2) nominate the party's candidate for vice president, and (3) draw up a party platform.

Party Platforms   Where does the Republican party stand on such vital issues as defense, education, and the environment? What do the Democrats think should be done in these areas? Each party gives its answers in a document known as a *platform*. The platform tells the voters what the party and the party's candidates stand for. It gives people an idea of what their candidates for president and vice president would do if they were elected.

Final Weeks of the Campaign   After the party conventions are held, the presidential campaign goes into high gear. The candidates give even more speeches than before. Much more money is spent on media advertising. Televised debates give the candidates an opportunity to argue their positions on various issues.

Early in November, the big day finally arrives—election day. Choosing between Democrats and Republicans, Ohio's thousands of voters mark their ballots for governor, U.S. president, and other offices.

TEST YOURSELF

The following questions refer to information presented on pages 91–94.

1. Define each term: *political party, nomination, primary, platform.*

2. How do political parties provide a choice in governmental leadership?

3. In a campaign for governor, what is the main difference between primary elections in the spring and the general election in the fall?

After the Election

Victory! You defeated Sam Sandusky by just 18,000 votes. Now as you look ahead to taking office in January, you know that political parties are certain to play a crucial role in your governorship. Many Republicans who helped you in your campaign will now expect to have some influence in the state government. They will expect you to listen to their proposals for new laws and to give political appointments to people they recommend. In addition, Republican lawmakers in the state legislature will look to you for leadership. You expect greater support from the Republicans in the legislature than from the Democrats. That is because, among politicians, loyalty to one's party matters a great deal.

Voters will also remind you of the promises made by you and your party during the campaign. For example, the party platform may have included a pledge to cut taxes or to enact a tougher law on pollution. Now that you are governor, you will be expected to carry out the ideas in the party platform.

DEMOCRATS AND REPUBLICANS IN THE WHITE HOUSE SINCE 1933

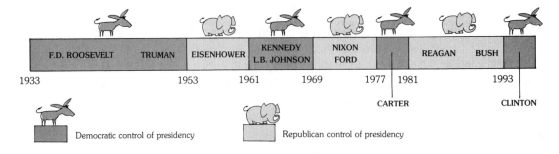

Third Parties

The Republican party and the Democratic party are the two *major* political parties in the United States. They are not the only parties, however. There are dozens of smaller parties that also nominate candidates and create platforms. These minor parties are sometimes referred to as *third parties*.

The Progressive party was one of the most successful third parties in U.S. history. In 1912, it nominated an ex-president, Theodore Roosevelt, for president. That year, the Progressives' famous candidate won more votes than the Republican candidate, President William Howard Taft. But the election was won by the Democratic candidate, Woodrow Wilson.

In 1992, a Texas business leader and billionaire, Ross Perot, won much public interest and support when he ran as an independent candidate for president. Thousands of volunteers broke away from the two major parties to campaign for him. Perot stressed the need to reduce a huge federal deficit (money borrowed each year by the U.S. government to pay its expenses). Although Perot did not win the election, his campaign caused the major party candidates, George Bush and Bill Clinton, to pay greater attention to the deficit issue.

In U.S. politics, third party candidates usually have little chance of winning elections. Even so, third parties can make a difference. Their ideas for government programs tend to be bolder and more original than those of the major parties. If the voters show that they like a third party's ideas, the Republicans and Democrats might borrow some of the ideas and put them into their own platforms.

POINTS TO REMEMBER

1 A political party is a group of politicians and voters who help each other elect candidates to office.

2 In a democracy, two or more political parties freely compete for votes and government offices. This process ensures that voters have a choice of candidates and policies.

3 Parties nominate candidates by holding primary elections.

4 At national conventions, parties present their ideas for running the government and dealing with public issues in a document called a platform.

5 The Republican party, the Democratic party, and minor parties (third parties) present different ideas in their platforms. By studying the differences, voters will better understand their choices on election day.

EXERCISES

USING WHAT YOU HAVE READ

The following statements (1–5) are all incorrect. Rewrite each sentence, changing the underlined word (or words) to make it correct.

1. In the <u>primary</u> election, the Republican candidate for U.S. senator was defeated by her Democratic opponent.
2. At their national convention in <u>November,</u> the Democrats nominated candidates for <u>governor</u> and <u>lieutenant governor.</u>
3. The <u>general election</u> determines which candidate for president shall be the party's nominee.
4. If you want to know the goals of a political party, you can read the document called the party's <u>campaign.</u>
5. In November, voters usually have a choice between candidates from the <u>same political party.</u>

CHECKING WHAT YOU HAVE READ

Match each definition at the left (1–8) with a term at the right (a–i). One term will not be used.

1. everything that a candidate does to win election
2. an election in which the voters determine who will be the party's candidates for office
3. a statement of a political party's positions on the issues
4. someone sent to a convention to make decisions
5. an organization whose members help each other to win elections
6. an election in which voters choose between candidates of rival parties
7. a meeting held to nominate the party's candidates for president and vice president
8. a party's selection of a candidate for office

a. nomination
b. political party
c. campaign
d. primary
e. general election
f. national party convention
g. delegate
h. platform
i. rally

THINKING ABOUT WHAT YOU HAVE READ

1. For democracy to work, do you think it is important that at least two major political parties compete for votes? Why or why not?
2. At one time, there were no primary elections. Instead of having the voters of a party nominate candidates, the party's top leaders would draw up a list of candidates. (a) What might be one advantage of the older system?   (b) What might be a disadvantage?
3. Meet with two other students in class as a "platform committee" of an imaginary political party. Give the party a name. Then discuss ideas that the three of you have for dealing with public issues. Write a platform for your party by presenting four or five ideas that all three members of the committee agree upon.

SKILLS: INTERPRETING POLITICAL CARTOONS

Elections and political parties are popular topics of political cartoons. One such cartoon appeared in *The Columbus Dispatch* in September 1992 and commented on the campaigns of the Republican president, George Bush, and his Democratic challenger, Bill Clinton. Notice that the cartoon consists of three main symbols: a bag of money, an elephant, and a donkey. Being able to interpret these symbols is the key to understanding the cartoon's message.

For each question, select the letter of the answer that you think gives the best interpretation of the cartoon and its symbols.

(Reprinted, with permission, from The Columbus, Ohio, Dispatch)

1. What do you think the donkey and the elephant stand for? (*a*) Congress and the president (*b*) the Democratic party and the Republican party (*c*) politicians in general (*d*) politicians and voters

2. What does the bag of money stand for? (*a*) world dictatorship (*b*) campaign expenses (*c*) powerful business interests (*d*) the U.S. economy

3. Why are all three cartoon figures making a V sign with their fingers? (*a*) all three are predicting victory in November (*b*) all three are attempting to hitchhike (*c*) all three are seeking to win the voters' attention (*d*) all three are playing a joke on each other

4. The bag of money is larger and happier than the other two figures. This image gives readers the idea that the true winner of the election will be (*a*) the Democratic party (*b*) the Republican party (*c*) the economy (*d*) a foreign dictatorship.

5. The cartoonist is trying to suggest that (*a*) the economy is more powerful than either of the major political parties (*b*) the economy will lead to a victory for both political parties (*c*) the candidate with the most money will win (*d*) big business will dictate the outcome of the election.

13

The Role of Public Officials

LEARNING OUTCOME: Understand the role of public officials in government.
a. Distinguish between elected and appointed officials.
b. Describe the ways officials can be elected or appointed.
c. Evaluate the actions of public officials on the basis of a given set of criteria.

Scrambled together below are the titles of various officials in the federal, state, and local governments. Notice that some office titles are printed only in capital letters. Can you guess what it is that the capitalized office titles have in common? The answer is

that the officials who fill these offices are elected; the officials who fill the offices printed in small letters are not elected.

Because our political system is a democracy, we might suppose that most government workers are elected to their jobs. In fact, at each level of government, those elected to office are in the minority. As you shall see, however, elected officials are in a position to set policy and exercise leadership. They are responsible for how well a government carries out its functions.

The government offices included in the box on page 98 represent only a tiny fraction of all government offices in the United States. Some 14.5 million Americans are currently employed by government at the state, local, or national level. In the state of Ohio alone in 1990, there were more than 100,000 people employed by the state government, more than 350,000 people employed by various local governments, and more than 55,000 people employed by the U.S. government. The total for Ohio comes to over half a million government workers. To say the least, government in Ohio and the United States is a huge undertaking.

After reading this chapter, you will know how to distinguish between those officials who are elected and those who are not. You will also know how to evaluate elected officials and decide how well they are performing their duties.

Government Workers in the Civil Service

If you call city hall, the person who picks up the phone is likely to be a *civil servant*. He or she was hired by the city government to perform a specific job for a certain wage. If employed by government, file clerks and receptionists are civil servants. So are police officers, fire fighters, health inspectors, sanitation workers, dog catchers, librarians, and janitors working in public buildings. Many of their jobs are like the jobs performed for private businesses. But instead of being paid a weekly or monthly wage out of a business's earnings, the civil servants employed at city hall are paid out of taxes collected from residents of the community.

The thousands of people employed by the state of Ohio are also civil servants. They work for different departments of the state government—Department of Highway Safety, Department of Education, Department of Health, and so on. Their wages come from taxes collected from the citizens and businesses of Ohio.

At the national level, more than three million civil servants work for the various departments of the U.S. government. There are U.S. postal workers who deliver the mail, FBI agents who enforce federal laws, treasury workers who mint coins, IRS workers who collect taxes, Labor Department officials who inspect the workplace to seek unsafe working conditions, forest rangers who protect the national parks, and countless others who daily perform a great variety of tasks. Taxes collected by the U.S. government pay for their labor.

Civil servants are *not* elected to their jobs. They are hired. Applicants for a civil service job must satisfy their would-be employer (the government) that they have the proper skills and training. Many of them are required to take an exam to determine if they know enough to do the work. Each level of government (local, state, and national) has its own system for determining who shall be hired.

Elected or Appointed Officials

The top jobs in government generally are *not* part of the civil service system. Top officials are either (1) elected to office by a vote of the citizens or (2) appointed to office by the mayor, the governor, or the U.S. president.

The three diagrams on the next page show who's hired, who's elected, and who's appointed in all three levels of government (local, state, and federal).

Notice that elected officials are at the top of each level of government. The chief executives (mayor, governor, president) choose, or appoint, the officials who manage the major departments of the executive branch. By far the largest group of officials are the civil servants who are hired to carry out specific tasks within each department.

Political Appointments   One room of the White House in Washington, D.C., is known as the Cabinet Room. Here the president meets regularly with a group of officials known as the *Cabinet*. Each member of the Cabinet is in charge of a different department of the executive branch of the federal government. For example, the secretary of state specializes in foreign affairs and directs the work of the U.S. Department of State. The secretary of agriculture, as the leader of the U.S. Department of Agriculture, runs federal programs for farmers. Because the executive branch of the U.S. government consists of 14 departments, there are 14 department heads who make up the Cabinet. They advise the president on the special problems and needs of their departments.

When choosing members of the Cabinet, the president considers a person's politics. A Republican president usually chooses Republicans to serve in the Cabinet. A Democratic president almost always appoints other Democrats. Cabinet members must be confirmed, or approved, by a vote of the U.S. Senate.

Besides appointing Cabinet members, the president also appoints many other federal officials including:

♦ *federal judges:* those officials who preside over U.S. courts and judge cases involving U.S. laws
♦ *agency heads:* officials who direct specific agencies or bureaus of the U.S. government such as the Central Intelligence Agency (CIA), the Federal Bureau of Investigation (FBI), and the Social Security Administration
♦ *ambassadors:* officials who represent the U.S. government in its dealings with foreign governments.

The president's choice for each of these positions must be confirmed, or approved, by a majority vote of the U.S. Senate. In addition, the president appoints personal advisers and assistants who have offices in the White House. Appointed to direct the work of these staff members is the chief of staff, a presidential adviser with considerable influence and power.

At the state level, the governor of Ohio has the power to appoint many top officials in the state's executive branch. For example, the governor appoints the tax commissioner, the director of highway safety, and 20 other officials who head the various departments of Ohio's executive branch. But unlike the U.S. president, the governor does not appoint all high officials in Ohio's executive branch. As you shall see in the next section, Ohio's secretary of state, attorney general, and a few other leaders are elected to office by Ohio's voters.

At the local level, the official who runs a city's executive departments (police department, fire department, and so on) could be either appointed or elected. If this

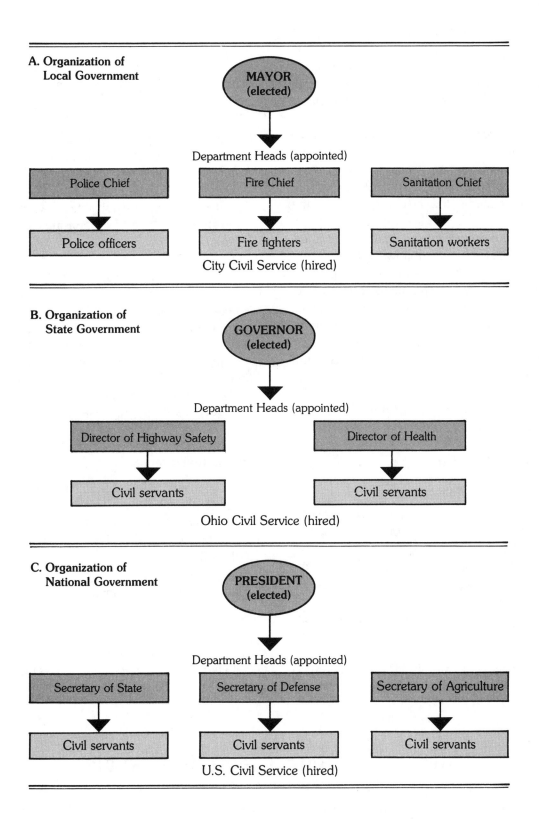

A. Organization of Local Government

MAYOR (elected)

Department Heads (appointed)

| Police Chief | Fire Chief | Sanitation Chief |

| Police officers | Fire fighters | Sanitation workers |

City Civil Service (hired)

B. Organization of State Government

GOVERNOR (elected)

Department Heads (appointed)

| Director of Highway Safety | Director of Health |

| Civil servants | Civil servants |

Ohio Civil Service (hired)

C. Organization of National Government

PRESIDENT (elected)

Department Heads (appointed)

| Secretary of State | Secretary of Defense | Secretary of Agriculture |

| Civil servants | Civil servants | Civil servants |

U.S. Civil Service (hired)

For each level of government, only a selection of departments is shown.

101

official is appointed by the city council, he or she has the title of city manager. If elected to office by the city's voters, he or she is known as the mayor.

In the early 1900s, almost all cities in the country had both an elected chief executive (the mayor) and an elected local legislature (the city council). Then in 1913, Dayton, Ohio, became the first large city in the country to adopt a system known as the *council-manager system.* Many other cities, including Cincinnati, followed Dayton's example. The city manager is an appointed chief executive—appointed by majority vote of the members of the city council. Like other appointed officials, the city manager is subject to being dismissed, or fired, by the city council if his or her work is found to be unsatisfactory.

Elected officials As a future voter, you should know the officials at all three levels of government who are elected to their jobs. Here they are:

At the local level

Mayor (head of the executive branch)
Members of the City Council (lawmakers for the city)
Members of the Local School Board (responsible for governing the public schools in a community)
County Commissioners (heads of the executive departments of county government)
Municipal Court Judges (Judges who hear cases involving traffic violations and the breaking of local laws)

At the state level

Governor (chief executive of Ohio)
Lieutenant Governor (in line to become governor if the governor should die or resign)
Secretary of State (responsible for keeping state records and supervising elections)
Attorney General (responsible for enforcing state laws against crime)
Treasurer (responsible for collecting taxes and paying bills of the state government)
Auditor (responsible for seeing that Ohio's financial records are correct)
Members of the General Assembly (Ohio's lawmaking branch)
Judges of the State Supreme Court (officials in Ohio's highest court)

At the national level

President of the United States (chief executive)
Vice President of the United States (in line to become president if the president dies or resigns)
Members of the U.S. Congress (the nation's lawmaking branch)

Notice that all lawmakers at *every* level of government are elected. Also, except for cities with city managers, the chief executive at *every* level of government is elected.

How to Evaluate Elected Officials

Is the U.S. president doing a good job, fair job, or poor job of leading the nation? How would you rate the performance of Ohio's governor and all the other state officials whom the voters have elected? Should they remain in office for another term or be replaced at the next election? A citizen needs to know how to make such judgments before entering the voting booth.

Keeping Informed Reading a daily newspaper is the best way to keep informed about government and the actions of public officials. News stories on a newspaper's front page and inside pages provide factual information about major political events of the day. You can also find reasoned opinions and commentary about current issues on a newspaper's editorial page.

To supplement information from a newspaper, you might wish to subscribe to a newsmagazine such as *Time, Newsweek,* or *U.S. News and World Report.* The articles in these weekly magazines give you an overview of politics in Washington, D.C., and issues in world affairs. You cannot rely exclusively on such magazines, however, because they say little about state and local politics.

Television is, of course, the most visual medium for reporting the news. Unfortunately, television news programs rarely present an issue in much depth. Information about an event is usually limited to a minute or two of images and "sound bites" (fragments of a longer speech edited down to a few words). Watch TV news for the purpose of seeing and hearing political leaders such as the president and members of Congress. It would be a mistake, however, to rely on TV news as your only source of information. Reading the news *and* watching it is by far the best strategy for keeping well informed.

At the local level, you can watch politics firsthand by attending the meetings of the city council or the local board of education. These meetings are always open to the public. At public hearings on local issues, citizens in the audience can participate directly by presenting their views.

Criteria for Evaluating Officials Your purpose in keeping informed about public officials is to be able to evaluate them fairly. Here is a list of questions you may want to think about when deciding whether or not an elected official is doing a good job:

♦ Has the official made an effort to deal with problems that concern you?
♦ Does the official have a reputation for telling the truth? (Or have there been reports of illegal dealings either by the official or those whom he or she has appointed to high office?)
♦ Has the official impressed you as being a strong leader and able manager?
♦ How well has the official responded in a crisis situation?
♦ Do you agree with the official's overall policies?
♦ If the official represents you in Congress, the General Assembly, or the city council, how has he or she voted on key issues?
♦ If the official has been appointed to run an executive department, has there been an improvement in the services provided by that department? (For example, have police services and law enforcement in a city become better or worse under the leadership of that city's chief of police?)

POINTS TO REMEMBER

1 The great majority of those employed by government are civil servants. Like applicants for jobs in private industry, civil servants are hired for their specialized skills and knowledge.

2 A large number of public officials are appointed to office by an elected chief executive. At the national level, for example, the president appoints Cabinet officials (the secretary of agriculture, the secretary of defense, and so on) to direct the major departments of the executive branch. At the state level, the governor appoints most department heads in Ohio's executive branch. One exception is Ohio's secretary of state, who is elected to office by the voters.

3 At all levels of government, members of the lawmaking branch are elected to office.

4 Federal judges are appointed to office by the president, but state judges are elected by Ohio's voters.

5 A city with a council-manager system appoints its chief executive—the city manager. A city with a council-mayor system elects its chief executive—the mayor.

6 In evaluating a public official, you should know your criteria (specific standards) for judging the official's record in office.

EXERCISES

CHECKING WHAT YOU HAVE READ

State whether each official is elected or appointed.

1. President of the United States
2. Mayor of Cleveland, Ohio
3. Chief of police of Columbus, Ohio
4. Governor of Ohio
5. U.S. secretary of defense
6. U.S. ambassador to Russia
7. Member of the city council of Cincinnati, Ohio
8. Chief justice of the Ohio Supreme Court
9. Chief justice of the United States
10. Member of the Ohio General Assembly
11. Member of the U.S. Senate
12. Member of the U.S. House of Representatives

USING WHAT YOU HAVE READ

A good way to organize information is to present it in the form of a chart. The first step is to divide a box into vertical columns and horizontal rows. Then label each column and each row. Study the following example:

ELECTED AND APPOINTED OFFICIALS IN THE U.S. GOVERNMENT

	Executive Branch	Legislative Branch	Judicial Branch
Elected			
Appointed			

Copy the chart on a piece of paper and complete it by filling in the titles of federal officials. For example, you would write "president" and "vice president" in the box under "Executive Branch" and across from "Elected."

THINKING ABOUT WHAT YOU HAVE READ

One criterion (or standard) for judging elected officials is whether or not they have kept their promises to voters.

1. Suppose that a candidate promises never to raise taxes and then raises them soon after being elected. Would you consider such action   (a) bad but excusable   (b) bad and not to be excused   (c) not a problem? Explain your answer.
2. Where could you find information about a candidate's campaign promises?
3. *Project:* Identify a particular issue that concerns you (for example: the environment, education, or crime). Find out what the current governor of Ohio promised to do about the selected problem when he or she was running for the office. Then write a letter to the governor asking what he or she is *now* doing about the problem.

SKILLS: ANALYZING AN ORGANIZATION CHART

A large organization consists of many departments and divisions. Each department carries out a different function and is supervised by a different boss (someone with the title of director, supervisor, or administrator). A good way to show how a public agency or department is organized is to draw a chart like the one that follows. This *organization chart* visually represents one department within Ohio's executive branch. In reading such a chart, you need to know that the top positions in the organization (those with the greatest authority) are at the top and center of the chart. Those in subordinate positions are connected by lines to the official who is their boss. If certain boxes in the chart are shaded, look for a key to find out what the shading means.

Study the organization chart on page 106 and answer the following questions.

1. State whether each of the following is elected or appointed to office.
   (a) governor
   (b) auditor
   (c) director of the Department of Highway Safety
   (d) assistant superintendent of the State Highway Patrol
2. What are the main divisions (agencies or bureaus) of the Department of Highway Safety?
3. What is the title of the official who heads the State Highway Patrol?
4. A captain in the State Highway Patrol takes orders from a _____, who takes orders from _____, who takes orders from _____, who takes orders from _____, who takes orders from _____.

5. Most departments of state government have *directors* at the top level, while *chiefs* run each major bureau or division of a department. Create a four-box organization chart showing these officials in Ohio's Department of Health:

   ◆ Chief, Bureau of Maternal and Child Health
   ◆ Director, Department of Health
   ◆ Chief, Bureau of Dental Health
   ◆ Chief, Division of Environmental Health.

**OHIO'S EXECUTIVE BRANCH AND THE OHIO
DEPARTMENT OF HIGHWAY SAFETY**

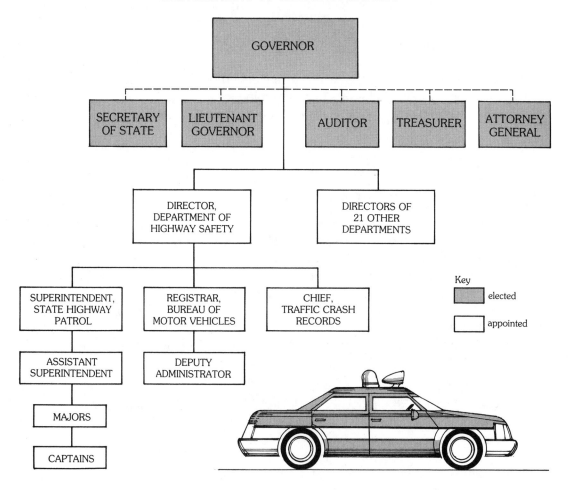

14

Knowing Your Rights

LEARNING OUTCOME: Know how the law protects individuals in the United States.

a. Give examples of rights and freedoms guaranteed in the Bill of Rights.
b. Apply concepts of justice, including due process and equity before the law.
c. Know the importance of a learning or work environment free of discrimination against individual differences.
d. Identify legal means of dissent and protest against a violation of rights.

How many of the following phrases have you heard?

◆ "freedom of religion"
◆ "freedom of speech"
◆ "freedom of the press"
◆ "due process of law"
◆ "the right to counsel"
◆ "the right to trial by an impartial jury"

These are just some of the rights guaranteed to every U.S. citizen by the Bill of Rights (the first ten amendments to the U.S. Constitution). What exactly is meant by "freedom of religion" and the other phrases? Why are these rights important to you and everybody else living in America?

You cannot protect your rights if you do not know what they are. Achieving this "learning outcome," therefore, will be important to you both now and in the future.

From this chapter, you will learn (1) some of the key rights and freedoms guaranteed in the Bill of Rights, (2) what "due process" means, (3) how discrimination violates a person's right to due process, and (4) what to do if you think your rights have been violated or ignored.

107

Your Constitutional Rights

First Amendment Rights As you learned in Chapter 1, the U.S. Bill of Rights (the first ten amendments to the Constitution) guarantees to every American a number of basic rights. The *First Amendment* contains some of the most important:

♦ *Freedom of religion:* Americans have the right to practice any religion that they choose. Governments cannot pass laws that favor one religious group over another.

♦ *Freedom of speech:* You may speak openly about any idea or opinion without fear of being arrested or penalized by government officials.

♦ *Freedom of the press:* The government cannot stop you from publishing your views in writing or broadcasting them in the media.

♦ *Freedom of assembly and petition:* You may join a group of other citizens who share your views. You may also request (or "petition") the government to change policies or laws that you dislike. The government cannot penalize you for joining an organization or signing a petition.

Rights of the Accused Other parts of the Bill of Rights—especially the *Fourth Amendment, Fifth Amendment,* and *Sixth Amendment*—prevent the police and the courts from acting in unfair ways. These amendments guarantee the following rights:

♦ *Protection from unreasonable searches and seizures:* According to the Fourth Amendment, law enforcement officials cannot search your home or other property without first obtaining a *search warrant* from a judge. The search warrant must list the exact place to be searched and the items or persons to be seized. In other words, the police cannot search anywhere and at any time they please for evidence of a crime. They must convince a judge that there is *probable cause* (good reason) for looking in the place mentioned in the search warrant.

♦ *Protection from self-incrimination:* Any person arrested for a crime has the right to remain silent and refuse to answer a police officer's questions. If this right did not exist, a person under arrest or standing trial might be tricked or forced into making a confession. That is why the Fifth Amendment states that, if you are accused of a crime, you *cannot* be compelled to testify against yourself.

♦ *Protection from double jeopardy:* Suppose that a person is charged with a crime, and the jury finds that person to be innocent of the crime. Can the person be brought to trial a second time on the same charge? No, the Fifth Amendment forbids a court from placing a person in *double jeopardy*—double danger of being tried twice for the same crime.

♦ *Right to a trial by an impartial jury:* A jury is a group of citizens who hear evidence in a court of law and decide whether or not an accused person is guilty of a crime. The Sixth Amendment says that the people chosen for a jury cannot have prejudices either for or against the accused. In other words, they must be "impartial."

♦ *Right to be assisted by counsel:* The Sixth Amendment also states that an accused person has the right to have the advice of a trained lawyer, or "counsel," and to be defended by the lawyer when the person's case comes to trial.

♦ *Other rights of an accused person:* The Sixth Amendment includes other guarantees. It says that a court that tries a person accused of a crime must

THE MIRANDA CARD

Before asking you any questions, it is my duty to advise you of your rights:
1. You have the right to remain silent;
2. If you choose to speak, anything you say may be used against you in a court of law or other proceeding;
3. You have the right to consult with a lawyer before answering any questions and you may have him or her present with you during questioning;
4. If you cannot afford a lawyer and you want one, a lawyer will be provided for you by the state without cost to you;
5. Do you understand what I have told you;
6. You may also waive the right to counsel and your right to remain silent and you may answer any question or make any statement you wish. If you decide to answer questions you may stop at any time to consult with a lawyer.

In 1966, the U.S. Supreme Court ruled in the case of *Miranda* v. *Arizona* that persons accused of a crime must be informed of their constitutional rights. For this purpose, police officers commonly read from a "Miranda" card (above) when making an arrest.

(1) inform that person of the charges against him or her, (2) allow that person's lawyer to call witnesses to present evidence in court, and (3) allow the defense lawyer to *cross-examine* (question) witnesses called by the government.

No Cruel and Unusual Punishments
Every trial must be conducted strictly according to the rights defined in the Fifth and Sixth Amendments. Suppose that a trial ends with a judgment of "guilty." Even then, the court must recognize another right. The *Eighth Amendment* forbids the court from punishing a convicted person in "cruel and unusual" ways. For example, that person can be sent to prison (a usual punishment) but cannot be tortured.

Due Process and Equity Before the Law

The *due process* clause of the Fifth Amendment may be the most important of all. It states that *no* person "shall be deprived of life, liberty, or property without due process of law." The right to due process means that a person accused of a crime is entitled to receive fair treatment from government officials. Furthermore, the procedures for arresting suspects and conducting trials must be the same for everyone. A poor person is entitled to the same standard of justice as a wealthier person. If there is discrimination in a courtroom, then the accused person's right to due process has probably been violated. A court of appeals may then decide that a trial court's decision cannot be allowed to stand.

Another legal term that has almost the same meaning as due process is the word *equity*. In simplest terms, equity means fairness. It means that everyone—whether young or old, rich or poor, male or female—is entitled to the same rights and protections guaranteed by the U.S. Constitution. The laws of Congress apply equally to all Americans, without exception. In the same manner, the laws passed by the Ohio legislature apply equally to all Ohioans.

TEST YOURSELF

The following questions refer to information presented on pages 107–109.

1. Define each term: *Bill of Rights, double jeopardy, due process of law, equity.*

2. Each of the following clauses (*a–e*) comes from one of the amendments in the Bill of Rights. Identify the amendment quoted:

   (*a*) "Congress shall make no law respecting an establishment of religion, or prohibiting the free exercise thereof."

   (*b*) ". . . and no warrants shall issue but upon probable cause, supported by oath or affirmation, and particularly describing the place to be searched, and the persons or things to be seized."

   (*c*) ". . . nor shall any person be subject for the same offense to be twice put in jeopardy of life or limb . . ."

   (*d*) "Excessive bail shall not be required, nor excessive fines imposed, nor cruel and unusual punishments inflicted."

   (*e*) ". . . nor shall be compelled, in any criminal case, to be a witness against himself; nor be deprived of life, liberty, or property, without due process of law . . ."

Discrimination: The Opposite of Due Process and Equity

Discrimination is the opposite of due process and equity. Discrimination means that a person is treated better or worse by others simply because of some physical or social trait. For example, a 50-year-old applicant for a job may be considered "too old." Or an African American may be excluded from a private golf club whose members are all white.

The following list gives examples of discrimination. As you read each example, think of yourself in that situation. Why is each example a violation of your basic rights to equity and due process? How might each incident affect your life and chances of success and happiness?

◆ You live in a neighborhood in which your ethnic group is in the minority. One afternoon, you walk into a store and start examining the merchandise. Five other customers (members of the majority ethnic group) are doing the same thing. A store manager tells you to put an item down and not to touch anything else. When you ask why, she angrily orders you to leave the store. As you leave, you notice that the other shoppers are freely picking up some of the very items you were looking at.

◆ You have just celebrated your 30th birthday. After working ten years in a clerical job at ABC Products, you apply for a promotion. You have all the qualifications for the higher-level job. But you understand that this job has always been held by a person of the opposite sex. Sure enough, a less experienced and less qualified person is chosen for the job you want. The person happens to be of the opposite sex.

◆ You have just learned that a coworker is paid 25 percent more than you, even though you perform exactly the same type of work each day. Also, you have worked at ABC Products two years longer than the coworker and thus have greater experience.

In these situations, there *may* be a good reason why the other shoppers were favored over you and why coworkers received higher pay and were promoted to better jobs. But you may have lost out because of some physical or social characteristic that is completely unrelated to your behavior or ability. In that case, you can reasonably suspect that your rights to due process and equity were violated.

Forms of Dissent and Protest

As a citizen with constitutional rights to justice and equity, how do you go about defending those rights?

Individual Action As you know, the rights to free speech and free assembly are guaranteed by the First Amendment. That means you can criticize government offi-cials if you think they have treated you unfairly. You will not be arrested or punished in any way for honestly speaking up for your rights.

One way to correct an injustice is to call it to the attention of elected lawmakers who represent you. Write a letter of protest to your representative in Ohio's Senate or

In August 1963, some 200,000 people demonstrated in Washington, D.C., for the passage of civil rights laws and legislation to provide more jobs. (*National Archives*)

House of Representatives. Send another letter to the lawmakers who represent you in the U.S. Senate and U.S. House of Representatives in Washington, D.C. They are certain to respond to your problem and may take action on your behalf.

Your right to vote provides another remedy. If members of a group are aware of being treated unfairly, they can cast their votes against those officials who have ignored their rights. They can pledge their support to candidates who favor their ideas and campaign to defeat those who resist reform.

Group Action   Signing a petition is another way of joining with others to protest injustice. This right of petition is guaranteed by the First Amendment.

Sometimes when many people see that there is discrimination in their community, they decide to seek justice by acting together as a group. They share the cost of hiring a lawyer to act on their behalf. On their lawyer's advice, they may decide to go to court to force a government agency, a company, or a store to stop its discriminatory practices.

Finally, if other measures fail, a group of unhappy citizens could hold a demonstration in a public place and carry signs in a protest march. This should not be done on the spur of the moment. First, arrangements for the march or demonstration must be made with local officials. Also protesters must take care to follow the rules of demonstrating peacefully. They should not deface or destroy property or assault anyone. (The police have the responsibility of preserving law and order. They may break up a demonstration that becomes disorderly and violent.)

POINTS TO REMEMBER ━━━━━━━━━━

1 The Bill of Rights guarantees to all U.S. citizens a large number of rights, including freedom of religion, freedom of speech, freedom of assembly, and due process of law.

2 Special rights apply to a person accused of a crime. For example, the accused person has the right to a trial by an impartial jury and the right to receive the expert advice of a lawyer.

3 The right to due process means that fair procedures must be followed by the courts and by government officials in their dealings with citizens. Such procedures apply to everybody equally.

4 If you feel that you are being discriminated against, you can defend your rights in a number of ways. You can write letters of protest to government officials. You can vote for candidates who promise to put things right. You can join with others in a nonviolent demonstration.

EXERCISES

On a separate sheet of paper, write the numbers 1 through 8. Then for each of the following actions, identify the letter of the amendment that guarantees a person's freedom to act in that way. Choose from the following answers:

a. First Amendment
b. Fourth Amendment

c. Fifth Amendment
d. Sixth Amendment

_____ 1. A family attends a new church in the community.

_____ 2. A homeless man arrested on a robbery charge demands that the state provide him with a lawyer.

_____ 3. A woman refuses to allow a police officer to search her garage because the officer has no search warrant.

_____ 4. A newspaper publishes an editorial that bitterly criticizes the president's foreign policy.

_____ 5. One hundred students take part in a demonstration protesting a local school board's decision.

_____ 6. A woman arrested for shoplifting refuses to answer a police officer's questions.

_____ 7. A student signs her name to a petition on an environmental issue.

_____ 8. After a jury finds her "not guilty" on a murder charge, a woman knows that she will not have to face a second trial.

USING WHAT YOU HAVE READ

1. Your family and several of your neighbors are opposed to the construction of an airport near your home. Make a list of the various legal means of dissent that you could use to try to stop the project. (You might get together with two or three other students to draw up a combined list.)
2. Look through your local newspaper and national newsmagazines for a week or two. Take notes on, clip, or make photocopies of articles about discrimination. Write a summary of each article, explaining how the people described reacted to the discrimination.

THINKING ABOUT WHAT YOU HAVE READ

1. Select one of the rights found in the First Amendment. Then write a brief story in which a government official violates a person's rights and that person argues in court that his or her First Amendment rights have been violated.
2. Based on your reading of this lesson, think of an imaginary situation in which someone has been denied *due process of law* or *equity before the law*. In a paragraph or two, describe the situation. Then write an additional paragraph in which you explain the best way for the victim in your story to handle the problem.

SKILLS: ANALYZING A DOCUMENT

Many parts of the U.S. Constitution, including the Bill of Rights, contain long sentences with several clauses. The Fifth Amendment, quoted below, is an example:

AMENDMENT V

No person shall be held to answer for a capital, or otherwise infamous, crime, unless on a presentment or indictment of a grand jury, except in cases arising in the land or naval forces, or in the militia, when in actual service in time of war or public danger; nor shall any person be subject for the same offense to be twice put in jeopardy of life or limb; nor shall be compelled, in any criminal case, to be a witness against himself; nor be deprived of life, liberty, or property, without due process of law; nor shall private property be taken for public use, without just compensation.

To understand the full meaning of a long and complex sentence like this, you need to break it down into its several parts. Punctuation often provides a strong clue to the structure of a sentence. The semicolons in the Fifth Amendment enable the reader to see that it contains five main provisions that begin like this:

(1) "No person shall be held to answer . . ."
(2) "nor shall any person be subject . . ."
(3) "nor shall be compelled . . ."
(4) "nor be deprived of life, liberty, or property . . ."
(5) "nor shall private property be taken . . ."

On a separate sheet of paper, copy phrases 1–5. Complete each phrase by writing *in your own words* what each part of the amendment is saying. Use a dictionary to look up the meaning of unfamiliar terms. (If you cannot express the full meaning of a clause in one sentence, you may use two or more sentences.) Your goal is to express yourself in plain, clear language so that any reader could understand your meaning.

15

Exercising Your Right to Vote

LEARNING OUTCOME: Know that voting is both a privilege and a responsibility of U.S. citizenship.
a. Recognize that property ownership, race, gender, literacy, and certain tax payments no longer affect eligibility to vote.
b. Identify the qualifications for voting.

In a democracy, people have the power to choose their leaders and lawmakers. Americans exercise this power on election day by entering voting booths. By marking paper ballots or pulling levers next to the names of candidates, they decide by majority vote who will fill the offices of president, vice president, governor, senator, mayor, and so on.

The U.S. Constitution gives "we the people" the responsibility of electing the president, vice president, and members of Congress. Yet the American people do not always live up to their responsibilities. Instead of taking part in government by voting, millions of qualified voters rarely

bother to enter a voting booth. In 1992, for example, only 55 percent of eligible voters participated in the election for president. That means that almost half the voters (45 percent) failed to take part. Bill Clinton won the election in 1992, but the millions who voted for him were fewer in number than the millions who did not vote at all.

On your 18th birthday, you will join the ranks of those Americans who are privileged to vote. What will you do with that privilege? Will you be among the millions who vote at every opportunity? Or will you be counted among the nonvoters or occasional voters? The information in this chapter should help you make your decision.

Americans Who Could Not Vote

When George Washington was president in the 1790s, the privilege of voting belonged only to a minority of the Ameri-

can people. Then, as now, state legislatures had the power to set the requirements for voting. In order to vote in the 1790s, citizens of Virginia, New York, and the other states had to be all of the following:

◆ male
◆ Caucasian (or white)
◆ owner of a certain amount of property—either land or money.

Some states also required voters to be Christians.

You can see that voting in the 1790s was a privilege granted to a minority of the total adult population. Women—about half the population—were disqualified from voting by their gender. Also kept from voting were thousands of Native Americans and African Americans (both male and female), who were disqualified by their race. Moreover, thousands of white males were disqualified by their poverty.

Changes in the Voting Laws

Removing the Barrier of Property   Early in the 1800s, the various states of the Union began to change their voting laws to enable more people to vote. The first group to be *enfranchised* (given the right to vote) were white males who had little or no property. Newly created states on the western frontier, including Ohio, permitted all white males to vote whether or not they owned any property. One after another, the older states in the East followed the example of the western states (including those created out of the Northwest Territory). By 1828, the year that Andrew Jackson was elected president, the property qualification for voting no longer existed in any state.

Removing the Barrier of Race   The next major barrier to voting was removed by an amendment to the U.S. Constitution. The *Fifteenth Amendment* was added to the Constitution in 1870 following the North's victory in the Civil War. The purpose of this amendment was to enfranchise African Americans in all states. It said:

The right of citizens of the United States to vote shall not be denied or abridged by the United States or by any state on account of race, color, or previous condition of servitude.

The phrase "previous condition of servitude" referred to African Americans who had been enslaved persons. (Slavery had been abolished in 1865 by another amendment—the Thirteenth.) Because of the Fifteenth Amendment, state laws that had previously allowed only whites to vote were no longer valid.

For many years, however, the federal government failed to protect African American voters in the South. They were often afraid to go to the polls (voting places) on election day—afraid that white mobs might attack them and their families if they tried to vote.

Two other barriers—the *poll tax* and the *literacy test*—prevented many Americans from voting, especially African Americans living in poverty in the South. The poll tax was a fee that voters had to pay to the state or county before voting. The literacy test was a test required of voters to prove that they could read. As requirements for voting, several Southern States collected poll taxes and administered literacy tests. Both requirements tended to be unfair to minorities.

The civil rights movement led by Martin Luther King, Jr., in the 1950s and 1960s finally persuaded Congress to put an end to discriminatory voting laws. In 1964, the

Twenty-fourth Amendment to the U.S. Constitution did away with poll taxes. Then in 1965, exactly 100 years after the Civil War had ended, the U.S. Congress finally enacted a strong voting rights law. The *Voting Rights Act of 1965* enforced the Fifteenth Amendment in areas where it had long been violated. It also abolished the use of literacy tests.

Removing the Barrier of Gender Both before and after the Civil War, many women were active in a movement known as the women's suffrage movement. *Suffrage* is the right to vote, a right long denied American women. Among the leaders of the movement in the 1800s were Elizabeth Cady Stanton, Sojourner Truth, and Susan B. Anthony. To attract publicity for the movement, an Ohioan named Victoria Woodhull campaigned for president of the United States in 1872 (even though most women at this time were not permitted to vote).

In 1877, Susan B. Anthony proposed that the U.S. Constitution be amended to guarantee women the right to vote. Time after time, her idea for an amendment was rejected by the members of Congress, all of whom were men. Gradually, the women's suffrage movement gained strength. Several states acted to grant suffrage to women living in those states. In most states, however, women still could not vote. Finally in 1919, Congress adopted a suffrage amendment. Months later, enough states ratified the amendment to make it the law of the land. According to the *Nineteenth Amendment:*

> The right of citizens of the United States to vote shall not be denied or abridged by the United States or by any state on account of sex.

The election of 1920 was the first in U.S. history in which women in every state could vote for president and vice president.

Voting Rights for Others One other group to be enfranchised was the Native Americans. Before the 1920s, the U.S. government had dealt with the Cherokee, the Sioux, the Wyandot, and hundreds of other Native American cultures as separate "nations." In 1924, Congress passed a law granting U.S. citizenship to all Native

This 1915 parade and dozens of peaceful demonstrations like it helped to bring about the adoption of the Nineteenth Amendment in 1920. What did the amendment say? (*Library of Congress*)

Americans. Along with citizenship came the right to vote.

The last major change in the voting laws was the *Twenty-sixth Amendment*, ratified in 1971. In the past, most states had required voters to be at least 21 years old. The Twenty-sixth Amendment lowered the minimum voting age to 18. That is why you can look forward to casting your first official ballot in whatever election follows your 18th birthday.

TEST YOURSELF

The following questions refer to information presented on pages 115–118.

1. Define each term: *enfranchise, suffrage, poll tax, literacy test.*

2. Identify four constitutional amendments that increased the number of Americans who could vote. Summarize what each amendment said.

Qualifications for Voting

To be a qualified voter in Ohio, a person must meet four basic requirements. He or she must be:

◆ a U.S. citizen (Someone born in the United States is automatically a U.S. citizen. An immigrant can become a citizen through a process called *naturalization*.)
◆ at least 18 years old on or before election day
◆ a resident of Ohio for at least 30 days before the election
◆ properly registered as a voter.

For native-born citizens, only the last requirement involves any effort. Registering to vote is a simple process, but many people neglect to do it. So long as they neglect to register, they will not be permitted to vote at their local polling place or elsewhere.

Registration involves nothing more than filling out your name, address, and other information on a simple form. (For an example of the form used in Ohio, see page 120.) The forms are available at various places: the offices of the county board of elections, a state Motor Vehicle Department office, a public high school, a vocational school, and a public library. You could call up one of these places and ask for the registration form to be mailed to you. You must return the form to the secretary of state's office in Columbus or to a county board of elections at least 30 days before an election.

Once registered to vote in Ohio, a voter stays registered for the upcoming election and later elections. However, you will need to register again if one of the following happens:

◆ You move out of the county.
◆ You change your name.
◆ You fail to vote in any election during a period of four years.

You can announce a change of address simply by calling or writing the county board of elections serving the county to which you have moved.

POINTS TO REMEMBER

1 To vote regularly in elections is a privilege of U.S. citizenship. It is also a responsibility—an action to be taken seriously as a matter affecting the nation, the state, and the community.

2 At one time, voting was restricted to a minority of the American people. But changes in state laws and amendments to the U.S. Constitution have given the privilege of voting to almost all groups in the U.S. population.

3 Today, the chief requirements for voting in an Ohio election are (a) being a U.S. citizen, (b) being at least 18 years old, (c) and being a resident of Ohio.

4 Qualified voters will not be permitted to vote in an election unless they are registered with the county board of elections.

EXERCISES

CHECKING WHAT YOU HAVE READ

Carefully read each statement below. On a separate sheet of paper, number from 1 to 6. For each statement, write either A, B, or C:

A The statement describes U.S. voting laws ever since 1790.
B The statement describes U.S. voting laws from 1920 to the present.
C The statement has never been true of U.S. voting laws.

____ 1. Requirements for voting have been made by state legislatures.
____ 2. Everybody living in the United States has been permitted to vote.
____ 3. Women as well as men have been permitted to vote.
____ 4. The Fifteenth and Nineteenth Amendments have guaranteed the right to vote to certain groups who had previously been prevented from voting.
____ 5. U.S. citizens who are male, white property owners have been permitted to vote.
____ 6. Requirements for voting have been made by the U.S. Congress.

USING WHAT YOU HAVE READ

Read the descriptions of the eight people below. Some would be qualified to vote in an election in Ohio. Others would not be qualified. Assume that today is election day. On a separate sheet of paper, make two lists under the headings (A) "Qualified to Vote" and (B) "Not Qualified to Vote." Write the names of the following persons under the appropriate headings.

1. BETTY is a 16-year-old high school student and a U.S. citizen.
2. ANGELA is a 23-year-old U.S. citizen. Two months ago, she moved from California to Ohio. One week after moving, she registered with the county board of elections.
3. ROBERT, a U.S. citizen, will celebrate his 18th birthday next month.
4. KIM is a recent immigrant, 19 years old, who hopes to become a U.S. citizen within the next ten years.
5. GLENN, an 18-year-old U.S. citizen, has poor grades and will not graduate from high school until the end of next year. Months ago, he filled out and sent in a voter registration form.
6. JENNIFER, a 25-year-old U.S. citizen, has lived in Ohio for only two weeks. Five days ago, she registered for the first time with her county's board of elections.
7. JIM, a 30-year-old U.S. citizen and registered voter, has not paid his taxes. Recently his house was seized by the government and sold at auction. Jim is temporarily living with a relative.

THINKING ABOUT WHAT YOU HAVE READ

1. Although voting is an important privilege and responsibility, many Americans do not vote. In fact, in a typical election, less than half the number of qualified voters actually go to the polls on election day. Why do you think large numbers of Americans do not exercise their right to vote?

2. Conduct a survey of voting behavior in your community. Ask ten adults whether or not they voted in the last presidential election. Ask each person to state his or her reasons for either voting or not voting. Take notes on what each person says. Share your information with other students in class. Do you think any of the reasons people give for not voting is valid?

3. Based on your survey (question 2 above) and what you have learned in this chapter, write a short speech urging people to register and vote.

SKILLS: REGISTERING TO VOTE

In Ohio, the secretary of state is in charge of elections. Assisting him or her are 88 boards of elections, one for each of Ohio's 88 counties. In order to vote, you must first register. A simple form that can be completed in a few minutes is used for this registration process. To familiarize you with the process, a sample voter registration form is printed below. Study the form and answer the questions that follow.

THIS FORM IS TO BE USED FOR NEW REGISTRATION, CHANGE OF ADDRESS & CHANGE OF NAME.	USE INK PEN OR TYPE
3. What is your birthdate? ___ Month Day Year	1. What is your full name? **PLEASE PRINT** Last Name First Name Middle Name
4. Where were you born? City State Country	S/D WARD PCT 2. What is your residence (home) address? Number Street or Road Apt. PHONE SEE NOTE FILED
5. Native ☐ Naturalized ☐ If Naturalized: Court City and State Date	City, Village, Twp. City or Post Office Zip
*See Note 6. Your Social Security No.? ___	PHONE DATE
7. What address did you give when you last registered to vote? Number Street	FILED ACT BY
City or Post Office State I have moved or will move on ___ Date	**NOTICE: PLEASE READ**
8. Complete for change of name only: Prior Legal Name	Your registration form must be **RECEIVED** by a county Board of Elections or the Secretary of State 30 days before an election at which you intend to vote. Volunteer registrars are NOT employees of the Board of Elections or Secretary of State. You are not legally registered to vote unless this form is received by the Board of Elections or Secretary of State 30 days before an election at which you intend to vote. **THE RECEIPT DOES NOT ENTITLE YOU TO VOTE.**
9. I declare under penalty of election falsification that the statements herein contained are true to the best of my knowledge and belief; and that I am legally qualified to vote.	
Signature of Applicant / / / Date	**THE PENALTY FOR ELECTION FALSIFICATION IS IMPRISONMENT FOR NOT MORE THAN SIX MONTHS, OR A FINE OF NOT MORE THAN $1000.00, OR BOTH.**
Signature of Registrar or Deputy Registrar / / / Date	NOTE: Furnishing your Social Security and phone numbers on this form is voluntary; their confidentiality cannot be guaranteed.

Note: Furnishing your Social Security and phone numbers on this form is voluntary; their confidentiality cannot be guaranteed.

1. When must a completed registration form be received by the county board of elections?

2. In addition to the board of elections, what state official may also receive the form?

3. Is it true that you must write down your phone number in order to complete the form? Identify the part of the form that supports your answer.

4. What is the penalty for making a false statement (lying) on the registration form?

16

Using Information

LEARNING OUTCOME: Demonstrate the ability to use information that enables citizens to make informed choices.

a. Use more than one source to obtain information.

b. Evaluate the reliability of available information.

c. Identify points of agreement and disagreement among sources.

d. Draw conclusions by reading and interpreting data presented in charts and graphs.

e. Identify and weigh alternative viewpoints.

When you enter a voting booth, you have a number of choices to make. Should you vote for:

(*a*) all the Republicans listed on the ballot *or*

(*b*) all the Democrats listed on the ballot *or*

(*c*) all the candidates of a third party *or*

(*d*) some Republicans, some Democrats, and some independents, judging the individual merits of each candidate?

To make your decision, you will of course need information about the candidates running for different offices. Where can you obtain the needed information? How can you be sure the information is reliable?

We live in what has been called "the In-

formation Age." Electronic forms of communication (the computer, television, and radio) are capable of providing vast quantities of information in seconds on any subject. But the speed and quantity of information does not guarantee that people will know how to use and interpret it. Vitally important to citizens living in the Information Age is the skill of comparing one source of information with another. Does Source *A* say the same thing as Source *B*? Do a candidate's statements in a television advertisement agree with statements reported on page one of the local newspaper?

A skillful and effective citizen is one who asks questions like these when making a decision. This chapter will give you practice in looking at different sources of information and thinking critically about them.

Sources of Information

As a voter, how would you find out about the views and qualifications of candidates running for a national, state, or local office?

During a campaign, information is widely available both in printed form (newspapers, magazines, pamphlets) and electronic form (television and radio). By reading a newspaper, you could probably find articles about the candidates on a daily basis. Turning on your radio or television, you might hear short excerpts from candidates' speeches on a news program. Or you might see or hear candidates who are guests on talk shows. As the election approaches, you can expect that the campaign ads for the opposing candidates will appear on radio and television with increasing frequency.

The Problem With TV Ads　Do not base your judgment of the candidates on just one source of information, especially if that source is a television ad. A television ad may be only 30 to 60 seconds long. That is hardly enough time to present the information that voters need to make a fair judgment. Furthermore, short political advertisements usually appeal to people's emotions. They tend to manipulate our opinions rather than inform us in a straightforward way about a candidate's record. In contrast, a televised debate between candidates can give viewers some idea of how the candidates stand on various issues. But do not suppose that you know enough about the candidates simply by seeing them perform in front of a television camera.

Newspapers and Magazines　Supplement your viewing of television by reading political news in newspapers and newsmagazines. Newspaper reporters are trained to present facts objectively—to state what happened—rather than to take sides. Thus, a newspaper's information about the candidates is likely to be more reliable than the kind of information contained in a television ad or even a television debate.

The skill of distinguishing among sources of information is important to *all* the decisions we make—not just our decisions in the voting booth. For example, if you wanted to buy a new car or stereo, would it be better to rely on (*a*) magazine ads for the product or (*b*) articles comparing various cars or stereos in a consumer magazine like *Consumer Reports*? Obviously the answer is *b*. On the one hand, the purpose of a consumer magazine is to evaluate products thoroughly and objectively. The purpose of an advertisement, on the other hand, is to persuade you that one product is "best" and that you should look no further for anything better. It does no harm to read and compare ads so long as you do not rely upon them as your only source.

Consulting Several Sources　As a rule of thumb, it is better to consult several sources of information than to rely on just one. Why? First of all, multiple sources are likely to present you with more complete information about a subject. (Facts omitted from a television show may be included in a newspaper story—or vice versa.) Second, multiple sources give you a means of checking the accuracy of information. What is reported on television may not agree with something reported in the newspaper. Or if the sources agree about a certain fact, then you can be more confident that the fact is accurate.

Identifying Alternative Viewpoints

Anyone who writes or speaks about a political issue has a personal point of view toward the issue. Therefore, when you look at different sources dealing with an issue, you are likely to encounter various viewpoints that disagree with one another. One writer or speaker may favor a certain policy while another writer or speaker opposes that policy. For example, consider the following statements by Speakers A and B. Each is speaking about a proposed law to fine pedestrians who jaywalk (cross city streets in the middle of a block instead of at traffic lights or crosswalks).

SPEAKER A: Jaywalking should be made illegal. Many accidents involving jaywalkers have occurred in our town. According to police records, 4 people were killed and 23 were seriously injured last year when they were struck by cars while jaywalking.

SPEAKER B: Our town has too many laws already. Citizens should be able to cross the street where and when they want to. The sheriff has more important things to do than to look out for and catch jaywalkers.

Notice that the speakers have opposite viewpoints. Speaker A wants jaywalking to be outlawed, while Speaker B wants jaywalking to be allowed. As a citizen listening to their arguments, you have the job of deciding how *you* stand on the jaywalking issue. Should you side with Speaker A or Speaker B?

Evaluating an Argument

As a person faced with a decision, how do you evaluate the arguments presented on both sides of an issue? How do you determine whether someone's argument is relatively strong or weak compared to an opponent's argument?

You should look carefully at your sources of information. Consider whether or not a source is reliable. A speaker's or writer's arguments may *not* be reliable if they display any of the following:

1. Opinions Unsupported by Facts An opinion is like a personal feeling or belief about something. Consider, for example, the statement "Ice cream tastes good." The speaker could just as easily have said: "I like ice cream." In either case, the state-

ment focuses on the person's feelings about ice cream.

As an example of a political opinion, look again at Speaker B's statement about jaywalking: "Our town has too many laws already." Implied in the statement is a personal dislike. In effect, the speaker is saying: "I disapprove of a town's having too many laws." It is a statement of opinion, or personal feeling, unsupported by facts.

What is a fact? A fact is any statement whose accuracy can be checked by research or observation. Two examples are:

◆ "Ice cream consists chiefly of cream, milk, sugar, and water."
◆ "Last year, our city council enacted a record 220 new laws."

Both statements are the type that can be proven either correct or incorrect. To *verify* (prove correct) the first statement about ice cream, you could either check an encyclopedia article, look up a cookbook's recipe for homemade ice cream, or call an ice cream manufacturer. To verify the second statement about laws passed by the city council, you could call the clerk at city hall. You may or may not actually do the work of verifying each fact. But at least you know that someone could do that work and thereby either prove or disprove a factual statement.

An opinion, on the other hand, is not subject to verification. How could you prove to others your personal feeling that "Ice cream tastes good"?

2. Sources Lacking Specialized Knowledge

Another question to ask about information is whether its author (or source) is known to have expert knowledge about an issue. We would tend to trust an article on heart disease if it was written by a doctor specializing in *cardiology* (the study of the heart). If the same doctor, however, wrote an article about jaywalking, we might wonder whether the author's information on this subject is completely reliable.

Whose statements on the jaywalking issue would you think to be the most reliable: (a) a member of the town's board of education, (b) a police officer who has conducted traffic on Main Street for 15 years, or (c) a novelist who has written five books? Why?

3. Sources Appealing to Emotion

Imagine that a third speaker on the jaywalking issue made this argument:

SPEAKER C: Can we ever forget the horrible accident on Main Street three weeks ago? How can we possibly forget Mary Jo, the ten-year-old girl who nearly lost her life and is now permanently crippled as a result of jaywalking? No, we will not forget nor will we wait any longer for the wimps in city hall to get moving on this issue. Those of us who care about the safety of our young people demand action and a no-jaywalking ordinance NOW!

Political speeches often attempt to influence an audience by appealing to people's emotions. An informed citizen, however, would know how to detect and largely dismiss comments that do nothing but arouse one's emotions. For example, Speaker C's reference to "the wimps in city hall" can be dismissed as an instance of *name-calling*. Speakers who call their opponents by different negative-sounding names hope to arouse people's anger, fear, or scorn. None of these emotions can provide a sound basis for making a rational decision. Therefore, whenever you hear a speech or read an article that uses emotional language, tell yourself to be wary. Think of the name-calling, emotional speech as *less* reliable than one that backs up an opinion with facts.

There is another flaw in Speaker C's method of reasoning. Because one person was injured while jaywalking, the speaker jumps to the conclusion that: (1) jaywalking is a common cause of injuries, and (2) a law against jaywalking would prevent future accidents. The speaker fails to consider anything but the one dramatic episode. Arguments based solely on just one person's case are generally weak and unreliable.

TEST YOURSELF

The following questions refer to the statements by Speakers A and B on page 123 and Speaker C on page 124.

1. On a separate piece of paper, copy (*a*) two sentences by any of the speakers that are statements of fact; and (*b*) two sentences by any of the speakers that are statements of opinion.

2. Which speaker does the best job of supporting an opinion with facts? Explain your answer.

Points of Agreement and Disagreement

People with differing points of view may disagree on some points while agreeing on other points. For example, in the argument about jaywalking, the three speakers may agree that at least one accident has occurred in town as a result of jaywalking. Even so, they disagree about the solution to the problem. Speakers *A* and *C* support the idea of an anti-jaywalking law, while Speaker *B* opposes the idea. In other words, people may agree on basic facts but disagree on how to interpret the facts.

Consider now the arguments of Speakers *D* and *E* on the issue of gun control. As you read their arguments, look for both points of agreement and points of disagreement.

SPEAKER D: To reduce the number of tragic deaths from gunshot wounds, we need tough laws regulating the sale of handguns. Each year, more than 10,000 Americans are killed by handguns. A substantial number of these deaths are either family murders, suicides, or accidents in the home. People may originally buy a gun and keep it in the home for protection against criminals. Statistics show, however, that guns kept at home are sometimes used, in fits of rage, against members of one's own household.

SPEAKER E: It is true that thousands of Americans are killed each year from the criminal and accidental use of guns and other weapons. But it is foolish to suppose that gun control could prevent such deaths. The truth is that growing crime rates in this country cause people to buy guns for their own protection. Their right to do this is protected by the Second Amendment of the U.S. Constitution. To be sure, accidental gun-related deaths in the home do happen. But accidents also happen on the highways, and nobody is proposing that we ban the sale of automobiles.

As you analyze these arguments, you will discover two points on which the speakers agree. What are they? (For the answer, see the bottom of page 131.)

Drawing Conclusions From Data

Often a source of information will include statistics, or data, to support an argument. Such information can be presented in a variety of ways. The most common ways of presenting data are as: (1) tables, (2) bar graphs, (3) pie charts (also known as circle graphs), and (4) line graphs. When presented with either a table or a graph, you need to know how to search for both specific facts and general meaning.

TEN STATES WITH THE LARGEST POPULATIONS, 1990

State	1 1990 Population	2 Percent Change 1980–90	3 Minority Population* 1990	4 Minority Percent Change 1980–90
Cal.	29,760,021	25.7	12,730,895	61.1
N.Y.	17,990,455	2.5	5,530,266	25.9
Tex.	16,986,510	19.4	6,694,830	37.2
Fla.	12,937,926	32.7	3,462,600	52.3
Pa.	11,881,643	0.1	1,459,585	13.3
Ill.	11,430,602	0.0	2,880,394	14.5
Oh.	10,847,115	0.5	1,402,493	10.4
Mich.	9,295,297	0.4	1,645,346	11.4
N.J.	7,730,188	5.0	2,011,222	30.7
N.C.	6,628,637	12.7	1,657,510	14.1

* "Minority" includes African Americans, Asian Americans, Hispanic Americans, and Native Americans.
Source: U.S. Bureau of the Census

Tables How would you find specific facts and general meaning in the table above?

The first step in reading any table or graph is to study its title. You then know the kind of information that it contains. The next step is to scan the vertical columns, noticing the heading for each. Now you are ready to pick out specific items of information by asking yourself questions like these:

1. Is Ohio included in the list of the ten most populous states in 1990? What was its population in that year?
2. Which state had the largest population in 1990?
3. What percentage of Ohio's population in 1990 was classified as "minority"? (Notice the asterisk [*] and read the note defining "minority.")
4. Did Ohio's population increase between 1980 and 1990? If so, by what percentage?
5. Which state had the greatest percentage increase in its minority population between 1980 and 1990?

In looking for general meaning in statistics, you are seeking to discover an overall pattern. Focusing on Ohio, for example,

you may want to find out how your own state's growth from 1980 to 1990 compared with the growth of other states. Searching the table, you might notice the following:

◆ Ohio's population grew very slightly (by only half of one percent) compared with fast-growing states like California, Texas, and Florida.
◆ The rate of growth of Ohio's minority population (10.4 percent) was well below that of most of the other listed states.
◆ Of the states listed, those bordering on Ohio (Pennsylvania and Michigan) also grew slowly relative to states listed that are in the South (Florida, North Carolina, and Texas).

Bar Graphs A bar graph like the one on the top of page 127 makes it easier for us to see overall patterns. Notice how this graph presents the same information as column 2 in the table. But the information is organized and presented differently.

The first step in reading a bar graph is to notice three elements: (1) the title, (2) the label or labels for the vertical axis (line) at

POPULATION GROWTH IN THE TEN LARGEST STATES, 1980–1990

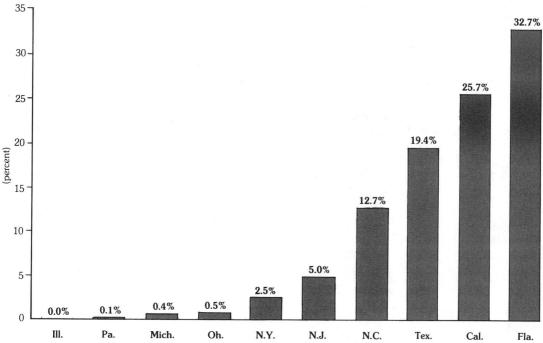

left, and (3) the label or labels on the horizontal axis. You are then ready to observe specific facts (example: Florida's population grew by 32.7 percent between 1980 and 1990). The arrangement of the bars from lowest to highest makes a pattern stand out. We now see clearly what was more difficult to see in the table. We notice right away Ohio's slow growth compared to that of states like California and Florida.

Pie Charts   Another type of graph, the pie chart, helps us to see the parts that make up a whole. In the graph to the right, for example, the complete circle represents what experts think the makeup of the U.S. population will be in the year 2000. The parts of the circle, as you can see, represent various age groups in the population in that future year. Of course, future numbers and percentages cannot be known with certainty. They are simply the best "projections" (or predictions) by population experts.

PROJECTIONS OF U.S. POPULATION IN 2000, BY AGE GROUPS

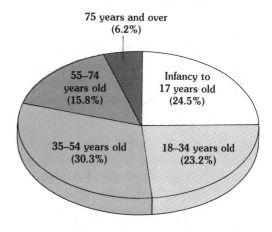

This pie chart shows the following:

◆ In 2000, the youngest age group (infancy to 17 years old) will probably make up 24.5 percent of the U.S. population.

◆ In 2000, the oldest age group (those 75 or older) will probably make up 6.2 percent of the U.S. population.

LIFE EXPECTANCY AT BIRTH, 1960 TO 1990 AND PROJECTIONS TO 2010

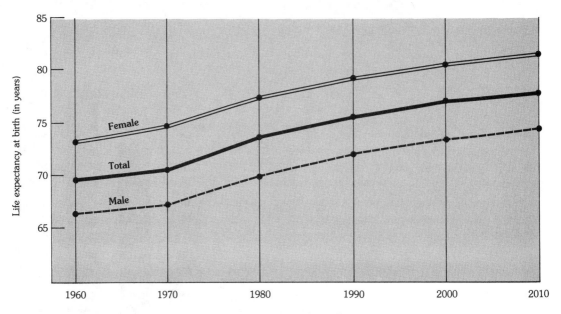

Source: U.S. Department of Commerce, Bureau of Census

What patterns, or general meaning, can we find in a pie chart? Usually, what stands out most clearly are the differences between the largest slice of the "pie" and the smallest slice. We see immediately that:

◆ The largest age group in the population will be people between the ages of 35 and 54.
◆ The smallest age group in the population will be people 75 or older.

Line Graphs   The kind of graph that is best for showing trends in data (increases and decreases over a period of time) is the line graph.

How can you find both specific facts and general meaning in a line graph like the one above? As with all graphs and tables, you get ready to interpret the graph by looking at key elements. First, you read the title. Next, you look at the labels for the graph's vertical axis at the left (65 years, 75 years. . .). Then you examine the dates running along the bottom of the graph

(from the starting date—1960—to the end date—2010). Only after surveying these elements are you ready to study the lines in the center of the graph.

Notice that this graph has three lines: a heavy solid line for the total population, a double line for the female part of the population, and a dashed line for the male part. Notice also that each of the three lines moves upward from the left-hand dot (for 1960) to the right-hand dot (for 2010). This fact gives you the graph's main message: that life expectancy for men and women in the United States has gone up since 1960 and probably will continue to go up into the next century.

TEST YOURSELF

Test your skill at interpreting information in a line graph by answering the following questions. (All questions refer to the graph on this page.)

1. What was the life expectancy of a girl born in 1960?

2. What was the left expectancy of a boy born in 1970?

3. What will be the life expectancy of (a) a girl born in 2010 and (b) a boy born in 2010?

4. In general, has the gap in life expectancy between male Americans and female Americans increased, decreased, or remained about the same since 1960?

POINTS TO REMEMBER

1 Before making a decision, you should look at several sources of information, not just one source. Voters need to make a point of seeking information from news-paper and magazine articles as well as from news shows on radio and television.

2 When listening to a campaign speech or reading a political article, be alert to the speaker's or writer's point of view.

3 Some sources of information are more reliable than others. Be suspicious of anyone who (a) offers no facts to support an opinion, (b) has little or no personal knowledge of the subject, and (c) attempts to arouse people's emotions rather than speaks to their reason and judgment.

4 Statistical information, or data, can be presented in a variety of ways. The form of information may be a table, a bar graph, a pie chart, or a line graph.

5 In studying any graph, look for both specific facts and general meaning (patterns, trends).

EXERCISES

CHECKING WHAT YOU HAVE READ

Answer the following questions by looking at the table and graphs on pages 126–128.

1. What percentage of the U.S. population in 2000 is expected to be young adults (ages 18 to 34)?
2. Between 1980 and 1990, how much did the minority population of New Jersey grow?
3. Name four states whose population grew by less than one percent from 1980 to 1990.
4. If both were born in 1980, how many more years could a female baby expect to live than a male baby?
5. What type of graph would be best for showing changes in Ohio's total population from 1900 to the present?

USING WHAT YOU HAVE READ

Joan Dokes is running for a U.S. Senate seat. For each source of information about Dokes, state whether you think it is a reliable source for evaluating Dokes's qualifications for office. For each source, answer either "reliable" or "unreliable" and give your reasons.

1. a speech by Dokes's opponent calling Dokes a "liar and fraud"
2. an advertisement for Dokes that speaks of her "courageous record on issues that matter"
3. a newspaper article describing Dokes's political record
4. a TV talk show in which Dokes responds to reporters' questions

THINKING ABOUT WHAT YOU HAVE READ

Read the four statements in the following political speech:

(1) Because elderly Americans have greater health problems than younger people, we can expect the costs of health care to reach staggering levels in the next decade as more and more people enter their sixties, seventies, and eighties. (2) Before the end of the century, we can expect elderly Americans over the age of 65 to outnumber all other age groups. (3) Population experts tell us that the average child born in the year 2000 can expect to live ten years longer than a child born in 1960. (4) It is frightening to think of the crisis that will soon overwhelm the health care industry unless we act now to do something about it.

Write a brief essay commenting on the speaker's arguments. In your essay, state whether or not the speaker supports an opinion with facts. If facts are used, identify them and discuss whether each is accurate. (Refer to the table and graphs on pages 126–128.)

SKILLS: SUPPORTING ARGUMENTS WITH FACTS

You may have seen news reports on television or read articles in a newsmagazine about the millions of tons of solid wastes, or garbage, that U.S. households and businesses produce every year. Imagine that you are now convinced that the garbage buildup is seriously endangering the environment. You believe further that there should be a federal law requiring Americans to sort their garbage so that more of it can be recycled.

The following facts about pollution and environmental laws may or may not support your views about recycling. As you read, pick out those facts that would help you build a case for stronger recycling laws.

◆ Every American produces an average of four pounds of garbage every day. The amount of garbage generated in the United States each year (more than 170 million metric tons) would be enough to fill a line of garbage trucks that encircles the Earth five times.
◆ Recycling can be expensive. Forcing businesses to recycle their wastes could cause many of them to go out of business.

◆ Paper accounts for about 40 percent of household and office trash by weight. Only about one-quarter of used (discarded) paper is currently recycled. The rest is either burned or dumped into landfills.

◆ California has a law requiring new buses and rental cars to use methanol instead of gasoline as the fuel.

◆ Although Americans recycled 56 billion beverage cans in 1990, this figure represented only about 60 percent of all discarded beverage cans.

◆ Only 1 percent of plastic wastes and 12 percent of glass wastes were recycled in 1988.

◆ *Waste Age* magazine estimates that it would be possible for an American community to recycle as much as 50 percent of its garbage. Currently, the average community recycles only about 13 percent of its garbage.

Write a letter to the editor of your local newspaper in which you (1) state your position about the garbage crisis and (2) support your position with facts selected from the above list.

Answer to question on page 125:
    Both speakers D and E agree that   (1) handguns have been involved in the deaths of thousands of Americans, and   (2) many gun-related deaths in the home are the result of accidents.

17

Becoming an Actively Involved Citizen

LEARNING OUTCOME: Identify opportunities for involvement in civic activities.

Most of what you have read in this book is about the knowledge needed to be a good citizen. For example, you have learned about the functions of the three branches of government and the rights guaranteed in the Bill of Rights. Being a good citizen, however, requires more than just knowing about government. It also involves all of the following:

1. voting in elections
2. keeping informed about current issues and public officials
3. participating in civic activities.

In Chapters 15 and 16, you learned about the importance of voting and keep-ing informed. In this chapter, you will learn about participating in civic activities—the third requirement for being an actively involved citizen.

What is a "civic activity"? Is it the task of paying one's taxes and obeying other laws? No, these are your legal obligations as a citizen. Government can penalize you for not fulfilling these obligations. A civic activity is a voluntary act of community service. Such service, given without pay, benefits the entire community, not just oneself or one's own family. The idea of community service is to give back something to the community to make it a better place in which to live.

Examples of Active Involvement

Let us suppose that one of your neigh-bors is campaigning for a seat on the city council. You have agreed to help out with the campaign.

Participating in a Political Cam-paign Listed below are ten activities re-lated to a political campaign. Which activi-ties would you regard as *passive* ones, and

132

which are truly *active*? (To be passive is to be acted upon by outside influences. To be active is to take action yourself.)

1. reading newspaper articles about the campaign
2. watching your favorite candidate debate opponents on a TV news show
3. discussing the election with a parent or guardian
4. answering an interviewer's questions in a telephone survey of voter opinion
5. attending a city council meeting to protest the council's policies
6. passing out campaign literature door to door
7. writing a letter to the editor of the newspaper about the upcoming election
8. volunteering to work a candidate's phone bank
9. helping to organize a rally for your favorite candidate
10. mailing campaign literature to friends

Activities 1–4 are important, but they do not qualify as examples of civic activity and involvement. Only items 5–10 are examples of active participation in politics and government. They qualify as civic activities because a person must make a commitment of time and effort to some public cause.

Caring for the Environment   There is an expression: "Think globally; act locally." It means that your efforts to protect the environment in your local community will have an impact on the larger environment of the state, the nation, and the entire world. After all, air and water recognize no political boundaries. Pollution in one place spreads out to affect larger and larger areas.

What kinds of problems does your community have in controlling pollution? Perhaps you have some ideas about how you and your classmates can actively help to clean up the local environment. You might want to organize a community-wide "litter roundup." On a certain day or weekend, volunteers could collect litter from roadsides, streambeds, vacant lots, and public parks.

Recycling programs are another way to take action on the environment. You might begin a recycling program in your school. You could organize a group of volunteers to collect cans, bottles, and newspapers and take them to a recycling center. This activity might even earn money for the school.

Taking Action on Many Fronts   What other projects can you think of for dealing creatively and effectively with local problems? Every year, in every community, both student and adult volunteers initiate civic projects that have a real impact on their communities. Here are just a few

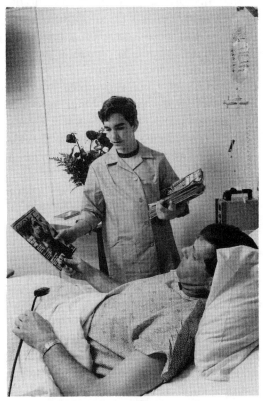

This young man volunteers in a hospital. Why is his action an example of civic activity? (*Copyright Billy E. Barnes*)

examples of successful efforts by younger volunteers:

◆ In Detroit, Michigan, a group of high school students became concerned about a poorly equipped city hospital. They formed an action group and collected signatures on a petition supporting the hospital's request for increased funds. When the city council held a public hearing on a proposed city budget, 500 students came to demonstrate their support for the hospital's financial needs. Partly because of the students' efforts, the council decided to give the hospital even more money than it had originally requested.

◆ In Seattle, Washington, students were alarmed by the news that the city council planned to build a garbage disposal plant near the high school. A group of students prepared a report describing the negative effects the proposed building project would have on the school. The report helped to persuade the city council to change its plans.

◆ In New York City, a group of students decided to try to stop other students from vandalizing school buses. Leaders of their student government and their school's athletic teams conducted a campaign within the school to discourage vandalism. As a result of the student

campaign, vandalism of the high school's buses ceased to be a major problem.

◆ In Lawrence, Massachusetts, students organized a "Jobs for Teens" program. Working with a state employment agency, they managed to find summer jobs for 300 teenagers. Impressed by the students' civic activism, adults in the community gave their support to the establishment of a new teen center.

◆ In Columbus, Ohio, a group of high school seniors became deputy registrars. At a local shopping mall, they registered new voters.

TEST YOURSELF

The following questions refer to information presented on pages 132–134.

1. Make a list of five problems involving either your school or your community. Select one of the problems and suggest a way that student volunteers might take action to resolve the problem.

2. Have you ever participated in a civic activity (project of community service)? If so, describe (a) the activity and (b) the benefits of the activity both for yourself and others.

Joining an Organization of Volunteers

A majority of Americans are involved in one way or another in voluntary efforts to help others. A survey conducted in 1989 found that an estimated 98.4 million Americans (more than half the adult population) were in the habit of volunteering an average of four hours a week to some form of community service. The following list gives

you an idea of the variety of ways in which citizens become actively involved:

◆ *religious organizations:* In a recent year, about 52 million adults spent time actively contributing to activities and service programs of churches, synagogues, monasteries, and convents.

◆ *educational groups:* About 29.5 million citizens volunteered time to support their local schools and libraries.

◆ *youth development:* More than 28 million adults gave their spare time to youth organizations, such as 4-H Clubs, Boy Scouts, Girl Scouts, Camp Fire groups, and Little League.

◆ *human services:* More than 25 million volunteers contributed to organizations specializing in foster care, shelter for the homeless, and direct services to the poor and the elderly.

◆ *health services:* About 21.5 million citizens voluntarily provided services to nursing homes, health clinics, crisis counseling centers, and organizations serving people with mental and physical disabilities.

◆ *arts projects:* More than 13 million citizens were involved in community theater groups, museums, orchestras, and other organizations for the support of the arts.

◆ *environmental efforts:* More than 11 million people helped out organizations committed to environmental protection and animal welfare.

◆ *political groups:* Almost nine million volunteers gave their time to the work of political parties and voter education organizations like the League of Women Voters. (See the list of organizations on pages 135–136.)

As you think about the above list, make some choices for yourself. On a piece of scrap paper, jot down the three kinds of volunteer work that you think you would most enjoy. Although most volunteers are 18 or older, there are many opportunities for a student like yourself to become involved in a community organization or service project. If interested in any of the activities listed above, you might want to

volunteer now. Speak to your guidance counselor about the opportunities that exist in your community.

Volunteer Organizations Listed below are some of the more famous organizations that rely upon the work of volunteers. To find out more about an organization, you might write to its national headquarters at the given address.

AMERICAN RED CROSS: Relies upon the efforts of 1.2 million volunteers.
Programs: Collects about four billion blood donations a year from voluntary donors and gives the blood to more than 4,000 private and public hospitals. Offers courses in basic, standard, and advanced first aid. Recruits teenagers to perform voluntary services in hospitals.
Headquarters: 17th and "D" Streets NW, Washington, DC 20006

BIG BROTHERS/BIG SISTERS OF AMERICA: Consists of 494 local agencies.
Programs: Assists children and teenagers who come from single-parent homes. Adult volunteers assigned to each child provide guidance, friendship, and support.
Headquarters: 230 North 13th St., Philadelphia, PA 19107

LEAGUE OF WOMEN VOTERS: Consists of about 1,300 local organizations. (Membership is open to both men and women.)
Programs: Encourages all eligible Americans to register and vote. Provides information about candidates and election issues. Selects certain local, state, and national issues for study and action.
Headquarters: 1730 "M" St. NW, Washington, DC 20036

LITERACY VOLUNTEERS OF AMER-ICA: Relies upon the efforts of 100,000 volunteers, all of whom must be high school graduates.
Programs: Trains volunteers to teach adults who have trouble reading, writing, and speaking English. (An estimated 27 million adults in the United States have this problem.)
Headquarters: 5795 Widewaters Parkway, Syracuse, NY 13214

UNITED WAY OF AMERICA: Consists of about 2,000 local United Way organizations.
Programs: Raises money for community service organizations and charities, such as the American Cancer Society, the American Red Cross, and the Boys Clubs of America. Relies on the fund-raising efforts of millions of volunteers.
Headquarters: 801 N. Fairfax St., Alexandria, VA 22309

YOUNG MEN'S CHRISTIAN ASSOCIA-TION (YMCA): Consists of more than 2,000 local YMCA branches, camps, and centers. (Membership is open to both men and women of any age.)
Programs: Operates health and fitness programs, child care, senior citizens' activities, educational programs for the disabled, and employment and leadership programs for teenagers.

Headquarters: 101 North Wacker Drive, Chicago, IL 60606

YOUNG WOMEN'S CHRISTIAN ASSO-CIATION (YWCA): The world's oldest and largest multiracial women's organization. Consists of 4,000 local branches. (Full membership is open to girls and women only, but men may be YWCA associates.)
Programs: Operates child care centers, classes on various subjects, food services, recreational activities, and health and job placement services.
Headquarters: 726 Broadway, New York, NY 10003

POINTS TO REMEMBER

1 Citizenship involves more than obeying the law, paying taxes, and voting in elections. It also involves the responsibility of actively and voluntarily serving the community.

2 Opportunities for civic involvement are extremely varied. You could volunteer to take part in an election campaign, help to protect or clean up the local environment, organize a student group to take action on a school problem, or join a service organization like the American Red Cross.

EXERCISES

CHECKING WHAT YOU HAVE READ

The activities below may all be worthwhile. But not all are truly civic activities. Write C for each statement that describes a civic activity and X for each statement that does not describe a civic activity.

_____   1. You volunteer to tutor young children after school.

_____   2. You write a letter to the editor of the local newspaper complaining about the need for litter control in your neighborhood.

_____ 3. You keep your yard looking great by mowing the grass once a week.

_____ 4. You return your library books to the public library on time.

_____ 5. You participate in a walk-a-thon for a community charity.

_____ 6. You volunteer at a recycling center.

_____ 7. You help your grandparents plant a tree in front of their home.

_____ 8. You serve as a volunteer at a senior citizens' center.

_____ 9. You join your neighbors in the cleanup of trash and debris in a creek near your home.

_____ 10. You take a paid summer job working in a hospital.

USING WHAT YOU HAVE READ

Find out how many of the organizations identified on pages 135–136 have local branches in your community. Call up one of the organizations and ask about the activities performed by its volunteers. Take notes on your phone interview and report back to class on your results.

THINKING ABOUT WHAT YOU HAVE READ

1. Why do you think civic activities are so important to the well-being of the community?
2. Should community service be made a requirement for high school graduation? Why or why not?

SKILLS: WRITING A PERSUASIVE LETTER

In a representative democracy, citizens have the right and the responsibility to express their opinions on public issues. One way to do this is by writing a letter to either a government official or the editor of a local newspaper.

The first step in writing an effective letter is to become well informed on the subject about which you are writing. The next step is to compose a draft of the letter. Make sure that you (1) identify the issue, (2) state your opinion on the issue, and (3) make a request for appropriate action. When you are satisfied that the letter's message is clear and complete, type or neatly write the letter by following the form on page 138.

Notice that this model letter is brief and to the point. It starts by identifying the issue. Next, it states the writer's opinion. It concludes by saying what the writer wants the government official to do. Notice too that the writer has been careful to use proper spelling and punctuation and to include standard elements of a business letter (heading, inside address, greeting, close, and signature).

Now, it is your turn. Write a persuasive letter to a local, state, or federal official. Or if you prefer, write a letter to the editor of your local newspaper. Use the blue pages of the phone book to find the addresses of government officials or the white pages for the address of the newspaper. If your letter is well written, you might even get a response. Good luck!

HEADING   1320 Duxberry Avenue
Linden City, Ohio 43302
October 14, 1993

INSIDE   The Honorable Paul Parks
ADDRESS   Linden City Council
104 Grasmere Street
Linden City, Ohio 43302

GREETING   Dear Mr. Parks:

IDENTIFY   I am writing to you regarding the building of the Linden Community Band-
THE   stand in Hudson Park. This issue will be debated at next Monday's city
ISSUE   council meeting.

STATE   As you know, we have many fine music groups in Linden City. However,
YOUR   most Linden City residents have not had the pleasure of hearing these fine
OPINION   musicians. Linden City simply lacks a suitable facility to accommodate
public concerts. The proposed bandstand in Hudson Park would be an
ideal location to showcase our city's jazz, classical, and pop music groups.
Hudson Park is a beautiful place that is used all too infrequently by the
citizens of Linden City. A bandstand would certainly add to the attractive-
ness of the park.

REQUEST I hope you will support the necessary funding to build a bandstand in
FOR   Hudson Park.
ACTION

                         CLOSE   Sincerely yours,

                         SIGNATURE *Marilyn Anderson*

                         NAME   Marilyn Anderson

Before sending your letter, make sure it has all of these elements:

◆ heading (your address and today's date)
◆ inside address
◆ greeting ("Dear ____:")
◆ body of the letter presenting your message
◆ close (either "Sincerely yours," or "Sincerely,")
◆ your signature
◆ your name, printed or typed.

APPENDIX

Taking the Proficiency Test

Taking the Citizenship Proficiency Test is an important event in your high school career. In order to receive your diploma, you must have enough knowledge and skill to pass the citizenship test (and the tests in math, reading, and writing).

How can you improve your chances of doing well on the test? First of all, you should review the 17 learning outcomes that the State of Ohio has identified as most important for citizenship. After completing your review, you should become familiar with certain techniques for taking a test. These techniques (described on pages 142–143) will help you not only with the Proficiency Test but with other tests as well.

Preparing for the Test

You need a plan for reviewing, or going over, lessons that may have been taught weeks or months ago. Here is a step-by-step plan that will help you review Ohio's 17 learning outcomes in citizenship.

First Step: Review the Outcomes Go back to the first page of the first chapter in this book (page 1). Read the learning outcome under the chapter title. Then slowly turn the pages of the chapter. Look at the chapter's headings and illustrations, which will both help you remember what the chapter was about. Conclude your quick review of the chapter by reading the "Points to Remember." Go on to the next chapter and the next and so on until you have reviewed all 17 outcomes and "Points to Remember."

Second Step: Review Key Terms Certain terms are crucial for doing well on the Citizenship Proficiency Test. Here is a list of these terms. What do you remember about the meaning of each term? If you are unsure of the answer, turn to the Glossary (pages 165–170 in this book).

Historic and cultural terms:
  Bill of Rights
  Cultural diversity
  Declaration of Independence
  Independence Day
  Northwest Ordinance
  Pledge of Allegiance
  "The Star-Spangled Banner"
  U.S. Constitution
Geographic terms:
  Compass rose
  Directional arrow
  Western Hemisphere
Economic terms:
  Capitalism
  Communism
  Interdependence
  Scarcity
  Socialism
  Taxation

Political terms:
  Absolute monarchy
  Amendment
  Bill
  Checks and balances
  Dictatorship
  Due process of law
  Equity
  Executive branch
  Federalism
  Judicial branch
  Legislative branch
  Lobbyist
  Override
  Platform
  Political party
  Primary election
  Representative democracy
  Separation of powers
  Suffrage
  Veto

Third Step: Take the Practice Tests   On pages 145–163 are two tests that are similar to the official Proficiency Test that you will be taking. Like the real test, each practice test consists of 50 multiple-choice questions. The questions test your understanding of all 17 learning outcomes. Take the first practice test as if it were the real test. Ask your teacher for the answers to that test. Note the questions that you answered incorrectly so that you can review information in this book relating to those questions. Then take the second practice test.

By carrying out all three steps, you should feel thoroughly prepared and confident of success on the day of the test.

Taking the Test

On the night before the test, make sure you get plenty of sleep. The next day (test day), be sure to eat breakfast. You want your mind to be clear and sharp so that you can focus on each test question. If you lack food and sleep, your mind may wander. Remember to bring *two* pencils with you to the testing site. If one breaks, you will have another in reserve. Sharpen your pencils, and you will be ready to go!

Starting the Test   You will be given specific instructions by the person who administers the test. Listen carefully to his or her instructions and make sure that you fully understand them. When the person says "Begin," do not start answering the questions right away. Take a few minutes just to look through the entire test. You will then have an overall idea of the questions you will be answering.

Managing Your Time   You are allowed to take up to two and a half hours to finish the test. Some students may finish after only an hour. But don't be afraid to take as long as you need, up to the two-and-a-half-hour limit. It is better to use your time wisely than to rush through the test and not do your best. There are no bonus points awarded for those who finish early.

Answering the Questions   All 50 questions on the test are multiple choice. Each question consists of a "prompt" and four possible answers. A prompt can take two forms. It can be the beginning of a statement, like this:

The document announcing U.S. independence from Great Britain was. . .

Or it can be phrased as a question:

What document announced U.S. independence from Great Britain?

Before answering, carefully read the prompt and *all four* of the possible answers. Do not choose an answer just because it may be a true statement. Even if true, it might not directly answer the question. Consider this question, for example:

In theory, a communist economic system is one in which
  A. *wealth is distributed to all individuals according to need.*
  B. *businesses compete for the consumer market.*
  C. *individuals invest in the means of production.*
  D. *society is divided into many social classes.*

Answer B is true of the United States and many other nations. But it is the wrong answer to a question that asks about a communist system. The right answer is A.

In each question, look for key words and underline or circle these words. (In the above example, you might underline *communist.*) Don't be afraid to write in the test booklet. Only your answer sheet will be looked at and scored.

Here's another tip for handling multiple-choice questions. For each question, cross out those answers that you think are incorrect. You may not know the correct answer to a question, but you can improve your chances by eliminating the incorrect answers. If you are still unsure what answer to choose, put a star or arrow next to the question and come back to it later.

What do you do if a question contains an unfamiliar word? Don't give up on the question. Instead, try to determine the word's meaning from the other words around it. You could also try to break down an unfamiliar word into its syllables, or basic parts. Often a prefix (start of a word) or suffix (end of a word) gives clues to a word's meaning.

Guessing   There is no penalty for guessing on the Proficiency Test. Answers left blank will be counted wrong. Therefore, you should answer *every* question, even if some of your answers are guesses.

Finishing the Test   After answering the 50th and last question, you still have some work to do. Go back and check any questions that you may have skipped and marked with a star or arrow. Consider each question again and give the answer that you think is right. Finally, check over your entire answer sheet and make sure that every question has been answered. If time permits, double-check your answer to each question. Remember, you have two and a half hours to finish. Turn in your test knowing you have done your best.

Good luck!

PRACTICE TEST 1

On a separate sheet of paper, number from 1 to 50. For each question, write the letter of the choice that best answers the question or completes the statement.

1. Which document serves as "the supreme law of the land" for the United States?
   A. the Northwest Ordinance
   B. the Declaration of Independence
   C. the U.S. Constitution
   D. the Articles of Confederation

2. The process for amending the U.S. Constitution usually begins when
   A. the Supreme Court proposes an amendment.
   B. the president ratifies an amendment.
   C. the two houses of Congress propose an amendment.
   D. the Ohio General Assembly ratifies an amendment.

3. If Ohio's governor vetoes a bill, which branch of government may attempt to override the veto?
   A. the legislative branch
   B. the executive branch
   C. the administrative branch
   D. the judicial branch

4. As head of the executive branch of the national government, the president is chiefly responsible for
   A. making the laws of Ohio and the other states.
   B. making the laws of the United States.
   C. interpreting both national and state laws.
   D. enforcing the nation's laws.

5. According to the preamble of the U.S. Constitution, who gives the U.S. government its power to make laws?
   A. the members of Congress
   B. the people
   C. the president
   D. the 50 state legislatures

6. Which is an unavoidable problem of all economic systems?
   A. Taxes are too high.
   B. A nation's resources are limited and scarce.
   C. Prices keep going up.
   D. Factories pollute the environment.

7. Laws about marriage and divorce are made by
   A. the U.S. Congress.
   B. legislatures of the different states.
   C. county governments.
   D. city councils.

8. Which of the following powers is exercised by *both* the federal government and Ohio's government?
   A. the power to declare war
   B. the power to raise taxes
   C. the power to coin and print money
   D. the power to regulate trade between the states

145

9. Which of the following best describes the role of a mayor in a city government?
   A. The mayor interprets Ohio's constitution and decides which parts apply to the city.
   B. The mayor passes tax laws to pay for city services.
   C. The mayor enforces city laws and regulations.
   D. The mayor decides which laws to carry out and which laws to ignore.

10. Which of the following has the primary duty of interpreting the laws of the state of Ohio in specific cases?
    A. the Ohio General Assembly
    B. the U.S. Supreme Court
    C. the Ohio Supreme Court
    D. the governor of Ohio

11. After a bill has been introduced in the U.S. House of Representatives, the bill is
    A. immediately debated and voted upon.
    B. sent to a committee for study.
    C. sent to the president for approval.
    D. immediately sent to the Senate.

12. Which statement accurately describes a representative democracy?
    A. Absolute power belongs to one person.
    B. Elected lawmakers attempt to serve the people who elected them.
    C. Only one political party is allowed to nominate candidates.

D. A monarch's powers are strictly limited by a written constitution.

13. Legal means of dissent include all of the following *except*
    A. petitioning the government.
    B. painting political slogans on the walls of state buildings.
    C. writing a letter accusing an official of being dishonest.
    D. bringing a lawsuit against a federal agency.

14. Which of the following documents was the first to outlaw slavery?
    A. the Northwest Ordinance
    B. the Declaration of Independence
    C. the U.S. Constitution
    D. the Bill of Rights

15. When U.S. automobile companies sell their automobiles in France, this trade
    A. helps the French economy but hurts the U.S. economy.
    B. helps the U.S. economy but hurts the French economy.
    C. helps both the French economy and the U.S. economy.
    D. harms both the French economy and the U.S. economy.

16. Some officials are elected, while others are appointed. Of the following, which is an *appointed* official?
    A. a justice of the U.S. Supreme Court
    B. the governor of Ohio
    C. the mayor of Cleveland
    D. a member of the U.S. Senate

17. Just before election day, Bob broke his leg. Although walking on crutches was painful for Bob, he decided to vote anyway. Which statement best describes Bob's attitude about voting?
   A. Voting is required by law.
   B. Voting is a responsibility of citizenship.
   C. One person's vote seldom makes a difference in an election.
   D. Deciding for whom to vote can sometimes be a painful process.

18. The main purpose of a political party's national convention is to
   A. nominate candidates for president and vice president.
   B. raise money for political campaigns.
   C. decide which bills should be introduced in Congress.
   D. increase cooperation between state and federal governments.

19. Which form of government would be most likely to guarantee basic rights of the people?
   A. absolute monarchy
   B. dictatorship
   C. autocracy
   D. representative democracy

Questions 20 and 21 refer to the map below.

20. If you were at location A, about how many miles would you have to travel to get to location B?
   A. 1,000 miles
   B. 1,400 miles
   C. 1,800 miles
   D. 2,000 miles

21. Location B is a city in
   A. New York.
   B. Ohio.
   C. California.
   D. Texas.

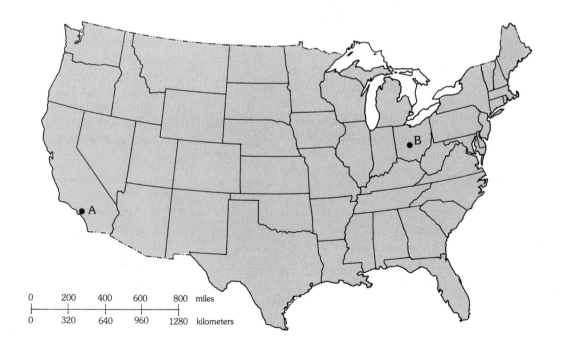

22. Another name for the national anthem is
   A. "The Pledge of Allegiance."
   B. "The Star-Spangled Banner."
   C. "My Country Tis of Thee."
   D. "The Battle Hymn of the Republic."

23. The United States has a culture that
   A. includes the contributions of a variety of ethnic groups.
   B. is based completely on English laws and customs.
   C. has hardly changed in the last 200 years.
   D. has developed without the influences of foreign groups.

24. A local hardware store was vandalized. Hardware displays were overturned, paint was sprayed on the walls, and a window was broken. To find out what happened at the hardware store, what would be your most reliable source of information?
   A. a professor of criminology at Ohio State University
   B. your history teacher
   C. your friend who had once worked in the neighborhood where the hardware store was located
   D. a store employee who had observed the incident

25. If you were arrested, you would have the right to
   A. automatic release after eight hours.
   B. bear arms.
   C. refuse to answer the arresting officer's questions.
   D. be tried by the U.S. Supreme Court.

26. The economy of the United States is best described as
   A. a communist system.
   B. a capitalist system.
   C. a command economy.
   D. a socialist system.

27. Government power is limited most easily in
   A. a representative democracy.
   B. an absolute monarchy.
   C. a dictatorship.
   D. an autocracy.

28. A major purpose of American political parties is to
   A. interpret the U.S. Constitution in specific cases.
   B. nominate candidates for different offices.
   C. carry out the laws passed by Congress.
   D. count votes on election day.

29. The largest percentage of funds for public education in Ohio comes from
   A. local and state governments.
   B. the federal government.
   C. state and federal governments equally.
   D. fees collected from parents of school-age children.

30. An Ohio law can be approved by the process of referendum. This means that
   A. the General Assembly must approve the law by a two-thirds vote of each house.
   B. the people of Ohio vote on the law.
   C. the General Assembly has overridden the governor's veto.
   D. Ohio's Supreme Court finds the law to be constitutional.

31. The manager of a community swimming pool makes it a policy to hire only male lifeguards. A woman turned down for employment at the swimming pool could argue that the manager's policies
    A. violate the First Amendment right to free speech.
    B. violate the principle of equity and due process.
    C. are a form of cruel and unusual punishment.
    D. violate the self-incrimination clause of the Fifth Amendment.

32. Community service is an important part of good citizenship. Which of the following is an example of community service?
    A. volunteering to tutor children at a local elementary school
    B. shopping only at local stores
    C. always paying your property taxes on time
    D. helping your grandmother mow her grass in the summer

33. "Due process of law" means that
    A. citizens aged 18 and over have the right to vote.
    B. citizens accused of crimes have certain guaranteed rights.
    C. the Senate must give its consent to treaties.
    D. citizens can practice any religion that they wish.

34. To be a qualified voter in Ohio, a person must
    A. be registered to vote.
    B. have been born in Ohio.
    C. have lived in Ohio at least a year.
    D. do nothing but show up at the polling place on election day.

35. In a socialist economic system, who decides what goods and services shall be produced?
    A. the owners of small businesses
    B. investors in stocks and bonds
    C. the central government
    D. consumers

36. Trade between Ohio and other states is regulated by
    A. the governor of Ohio.
    B. the U.S. Congress.
    C. state legislatures.
    D. treaties between states.

37. The stripes on the U.S. flag symbolize
    A. all the states of the Union today.
    B. the original 13 states.
    C. different ethnic groups who make up the American people.
    D. U.S. battle victories in various wars.

38. When the U.S. Senate and House of Representatives cannot agree on a certain bill, their differences are often settled by
    A. a conference committee.
    B. the Supreme Court.
    C. the president.
    D. a constitutional amendment.

39. Which of the following is an example of a civic activity?
    A. working at a local supermarket for a minimum wage
    B. volunteering to wash the dishes at home
    C. donating your services to a community recycling center
    D. regularly reading the newspaper

40. The following speeches present *two* views about a proposed new park in your community.

   I. "The park is long overdue. It will give us a place near our home where my children can play and where we can enjoy family picnics. Our community association conducted a poll last year that showed a majority favored this new park. Let's build it!"

   II. "The park would increase traffic in the neighborhood. Hoodlums would have a new place to hang out. The city may have to hire more police officers to patrol the park at night. In short, this park would just ruin our neighborhood and lower our property values. If this park is built, I'm moving."

Which statement about the above speeches is accurate?
   A. Speech I takes a neutral view of whether or not a new park should be built.
   B. Speech II consists of opinions that are unsupported by facts.
   C. Both speeches back up their claims with supporting data.
   D. Speech II presents a stronger argument because it threatens to back up the speaker's words with deeds.

41. Which graph might be used to show cultural diversity in Ohio?
   A. a line graph on economic growth in Ohio
   B. a bar graph on the immigrant population in Ohio today
   C. a pie graph on levels of education of Ohio's adult population
   D. a line graph on the birth rate in Ohio

42. Two people are running for political office. How could you *best* inform yourself about the qualifications of the two candidates?
   A. watch the candidates' ads on television
   B. study the campaign literature of one candidate
   C. watch TV news shows regularly for about two weeks before the election
   D. seek information from several different sources, including newspapers, magazines, and television programs

43. Cindy is arrested in a criminal case. She refuses to answer any questions about the alleged crime, claiming that she is "taking the Fifth Amendment." "Taking the Fifth Amendment" means that
   A. Cindy is pleading innocent to the charges against her.
   B. Cindy is too young to be arrested for this crime.
   C. Cindy has not had the opportunity to discuss the case with a lawyer.
   D. Cindy does not have to answer questions that might incriminate her.

44. The Bill of Rights guarantees all of the following *except*
   A. freedom of the press.
   B. the right to full employment.
   C. the right to freely assemble.
   D. freedom of speech.

45. The taxes collected by Ohio's government pay for which of the following?
   A. the purchase of weapons for the navy
   B. the salaries of civil servants in the FBI
   C. the salaries of justices on the U.S. Supreme Court
   D. the salaries of officers in the State Highway Patrol

46. Which of the following statements about voting rights in Ohio is *not* true?
   A. Laws passed by Ohio's General Assembly determine the qualifications for voting in the state.
   B. Ohio is responsible for holding elections for national offices as well as state offices.
   C. The minimum voting age of 18 was established by an amendment to the U.S. Constitution.
   D. Voters must pay a poll tax before being allowed to vote in an election.

47. Which of the following decisions are made at a national political convention?
   A. how much money the party will spend on campaigns
   B. what will be the party's positions on various public issues
   C. how many new members will be admitted to the party
   D. who will be the party's candidates for governor and lieutenant governor

48. The president appoints members of his or her cabinet with the approval of
   A. the U.S. Senate.
   B. both houses of Congress.
   C. the U.S. Supreme Court.
   D. the vice president.

Questions 49 and 50 refer to the map below.

49. Which point on the map represents the location of Ohio's capital?
   A. point *A*
   B. point *B*
   C. point *C*
   D. point *D*

50. About how far is point *A* from point *C*?
   A. 70 miles
   B. 125 miles
   C. 150 miles
   D. 220 miles

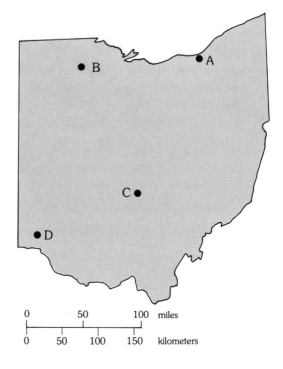

PRACTICE TEST 2

On a separate sheet of paper, number from 1 to 50. For each question, write the letter of the choice that best answers the question or completes the statement.

1. According to the line graph below, which of the following is accurate?
   A. Federal spending on education rose every year during the decade of the 1950s.
   B. Federal spending on education declined every year during the 1950s.
   C. Federal spending on education rose every year but one during the 1950s.
   D. The sharpest rise in federal spending on education was between 1953 and 1954.

2. Which of the following officials are appointed to office?

   A. U.S. Supreme Court justices
   B. members of the U.S. House of Representatives
   C. state legislators
   D. governors

3. The country of Discordia holds elections for president every six years. Only one person has ever run for office, and he has been the ruler for 16 years. He holds legislative, judicial, and executive powers. Discordia would best be described as
   A. a representative democracy.
   B. a monarchy.
   C. a dictatorship.
   D. a republic.

FEDERAL SPENDING ON EDUCATION, 1950–1959

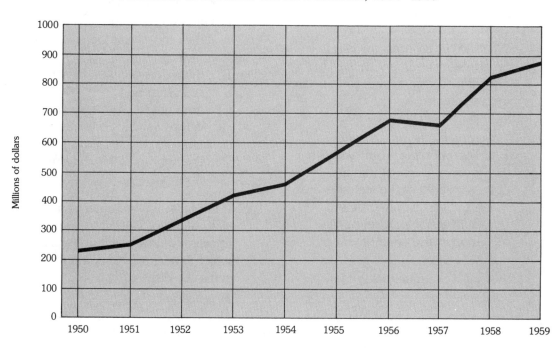

4. According to the map above, which letter represents the capital of the United States?
   A. *A*
   B. *B*
   C. *C*
   D. *D*

5. What action is necessary before a proposed amendment to the U.S. Constitution can be sent to the states for ratification?
   A. The U.S. Congress votes to approve the amendment.
   B. The Supreme Court votes in favor of the amendment.
   C. A majority of the state governors approves the amendment.
   D. Both major political parties support the amendment.

6. It is most accurate to say that Ohioans
   A. are of only one ethnic group.
   B. generally have the same views on controversial issues

C. are the descendants of several racial and ethnic groups.
D. are all descended from settlers of the Northwest Territory.

7. James was arrested for burglary. According to the Bill of Rights, he has all the following rights *except*
   A. the right to trial by a jury of his peers.
   B. the right to have a lawyer represent him.
   C. the right to cross-examine any witnesses who testify against him.
   D. the right to pick the members of his jury.

8. If the federal government and the state of Ohio disagree over how to interpret a new pollution regulation, which branch of government could settle the dispute?
   A. legislative
   B. executive
   C. judicial
   D. local

9. The United States flag contains one star for *every*
    A. president.
    B. senator.
    C. governor.
    D. state.

10. Mrs. Smith wants to build an addition onto the apartment building that she owns in Toledo, Ohio. From which government could she obtain the building permit?
    A. national
    B. state
    C. legislative
    D. city

11. Which of the following would be an example of active civic participation?
    A. working as an employee of the public library
    B. working as a city police officer
    C. organizing a neighborhood collection of food for hurricane victims
    D. working as a preschool teacher

12. Which of the following situations would make Tony ineligible to vote?
    A. He is over 65 years old.
    B. He is 17 years old.
    C. He is on welfare.
    D. He has not graduated from high school.

13. According to the map below, in what direction is City Hall from the Post Office?
    A. north
    B. east
    C. west
    D. south

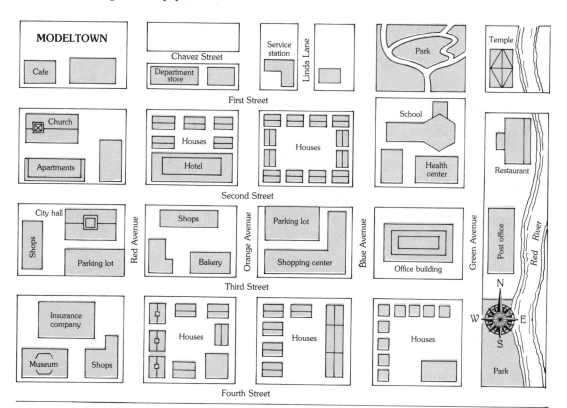

14. Tonya wants to write a paper for school describing the official platforms of the major political parties in the next election. Where could she find the most accurate information on this subject?
    A. in newspaper editorials about the candidates
    B. in TV advertisements for each candidate
    C. in newspaper articles summarizing the platforms
    D. from talking with neighbors and friends

15. Which of the following represents the diversity of cultures in Ohio?
    A. Many Americans vacation in Europe and South America.
    B. Many students in Ohio schools come from non-English-speaking families.
    C. Many foreign investors own property in Ohio.
    D. Many Ohio companies have plants or offices in foreign countries.

16. Mr. Smith will hire only young men who are at least six feet tall and very thin to wait on customers in his store. A group of young women learned about Mr. Smith's hiring policy, and they want to protest against it. Which of the following is a legal means of dissent that the young women could take?
    A. form a human chain to block customers from entering the store
    B. write letters to the editor of the local newspaper and file a complaint with the city government
    C. paint protest messages on the store's windows
    D. sit in the aisles of the store to make shopping more difficult for customers

17. The document that proclaimed the United States a free and independent nation was the
    A. Declaration of Independence.
    B. Northwest Ordinance.
    C. Bill of Rights.
    D. U.S. Constitution.

18. All levels of government in the United States assess taxes to pay for services. Which of the following is an example of a government service paid for by taxes?
    A. police protection
    B. advertising for department stores
    C. automobile production
    D. taxi service

19. According to the bar graph on page 157, which of the following is true?
    A. There was a greater percentage of poor elderly people than poor children in 1974.
    B. The percentage of poor children in 1985 was less than the percentage of poor elderly people.
    C. The percentage of poor elderly people in 1959 was greater than the percentage of poor children.
    D. In 1985, the percentage of poor children was equal to the percentage of poor elderly people.

20. Which type of government would have the largest percentage of citizens with real political power?
    A. monarchy
    B. representative democracy
    C. dictatorship
    D. communism

PERCENT OF CHILDREN AND ELDERLY WHO WERE POOR

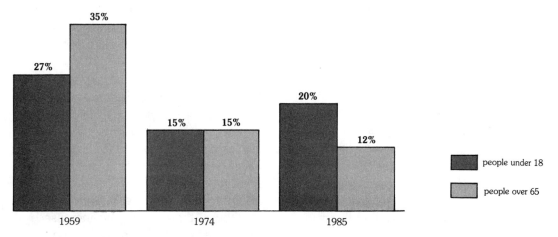

people under 18

people over 65

21. Which of the following officials are elected to office?
    A. chief justice of the United States
    B. city manager of Dayton
    C. members of the U.S. Congress
    D. president's chief of staff

22. According to the map below, which letter represents the United States?
    A. *A*
    B. *B*
    C. *C*
    D. *D*

23. The Declaration of Independence is the reason that U.S. citizens celebrate
    A. Labor Day.
    B. the Fourth of July.
    C. Memorial Day.
    D. Thanksgiving Day.

24. The president has just vetoed a new tax bill passed by Congress. In what way can the bill still become law?
    A. The Supreme Court can override the veto by a majority vote.
    B. Congress can pass the bill again by a majority vote.
    C. Congress can override the veto with a two-thirds vote of each house.
    D. Two-thirds of the state legislatures can vote to override the veto.

25. Monica recently moved into a new community. She wants to vote in the next election. In order to vote, she will have to meet all the following requirements *except*
    A. being at least 18 years old.
    B. passing a test to prove that she can read.
    C. being a citizen of the United States.
    D. registering with the Board of Elections.

26. Which of the following is an elected local official?
    A. member of Congress
    B. mayor
    C. member of the Ohio General Assembly
    D. chief justice of the Ohio Supreme Court

Questions 27 and 28 refer to the following reading passage:

A company proposes to build a new restaurant to serve boaters who use a popular lake in a county park. The restaurant would serve liquor.

Various residents of the county speak out against the restaurant. They say:

Liquor and boating do not mix. The availability of liquor would result in more boating accidents. A restaurant serving liquor would make the park less appealing to families with children. Moreover, there would be increased motor vehicle traffic near the park, which would create an additional danger to people in the area.

Other people favor the restaurant. They say:

The increased business would be good for the local economy; the restaurant would create jobs. Boaters who want to drink can get liquor somewhere else, whether or not this restaurant is built. The increased traffic associated with a restaurant could be controlled by improving the roads, building parking lots, and installing traffic lights and stop signs.

27. Based upon the statements above, on which of the following points do the two sides agree?
    A. Building the restaurant will result in an increase in boating accidents.
    B. There will be more motor vehicle accidents in the park if the restaurant is built.
    C. Liquor and boating do not mix.
    D. Traffic in the park will increase if the restaurant is built.

28. From what source could you get the most accurate information about the relationship between boating accidents and drinking?
   A. the State Division of Water Safety
   B. the restaurant owners
   C. residents around the lake
   D. boaters who use the lake

29. State officials want to increase the number of people who vote in the next election. Which of the following actions would NOT help them accomplish that goal?
   A. provide more places to register
   B. establish mail-in registration forms
   C. conduct an advertising campaign on radio and television
   D. shorten the number of hours that the polls are open

30. It is sometimes said that the United States is a "nation of immigrants." Which of the following statements best supports that view?
   A. The majority of Americans have passports to travel overseas.
   B. Most Americans are registered voters.
   C. The health of the U.S. economy is dependent upon trade with foreign countries.
   D. The ancestors of most U.S. citizens originally came from another country.

31. If Congress passed a new environmental protection bill and the president signed it into law, which of the following would be responsible for making sure the law was carried out?
   A. the executive branch of the United States

   B. the judicial branch of the United States
   C. the legislative branch of the United States
   D. the state legislature of Ohio

32. Robert was arrested for auto theft. He is 30 years old and has two prior convictions. Robert has no money, so he cannot afford to hire a lawyer. The fact that the state will appoint a lawyer to act on Robert's behalf is part of the constitutional guarantee of
   A. the elastic clause.
   B. habeas corpus.
   C. due process.
   D. federalism.

33. A legitimate function of a political party would include which of the following?
   A. arguing cases before the Supreme Court
   B. writing a platform for a presidential election
   C. ratifying amendments to the Constitution
   D. conducting diplomatic relations

34. Free enterprise and the profit motive are most closely associated with
   A. capitalism.
   B. socialism.
   C. communism.
   D. federalism.

35. The words to the national anthem were written during the
   A. Revolutionary War.
   B. Constitutional Convention.
   C. War of 1812.
   D. last 100 years.

SOURCES OF FEDERAL REVENUE

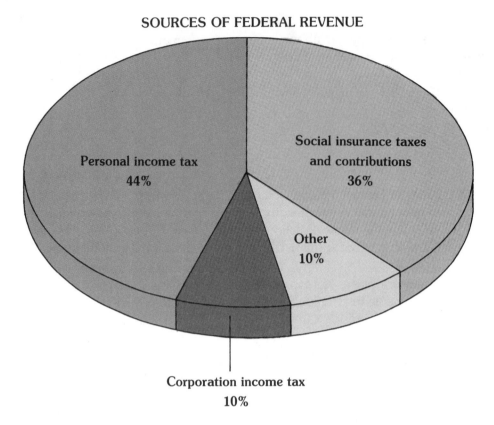

Personal income tax
44%

Social insurance taxes
and contributions
36%

Other
10%

Corporation income tax
10%

36. Which of the following was an act of Congress that set up rules for governing U.S. lands that had not yet become states?
   A. U.S. Constitution
   B. Declaration of Independence
   C. Bill of Rights
   D. Northwest Ordinance

37. Thomas took a job in a factory that manufactures lighting fixtures. During the first year, he saved 10 percent of his pay. At the end of that year, he also received a profit-sharing bonus. He used the money that he saved to make a down payment on a car, and he invested the profit-sharing check in the stock market. Thomas most likely lives under what kind of economic system?
   A. socialism
   B. communism
   C. capitalism
   D. monarchy

38. According to the pie chart above, which of the following statements is true?
   A. Corporation taxes make up a greater percentage of federal income than any other source.
   B. Personal income taxes make up the single largest source of federal income.
   C. Corporation income taxes plus "other" sources of federal revenue are greater than social insurance taxes and contributions.
   D. Social Security taxes make up the single largest percentage of federal revenue.

39. A federal law may be ruled unconstitutional when
    A. two-thirds of the state legislatures vote against it.
    B. the Supreme Court declares it unconstitutional.
    C. the president vetoes it.
    D. a majority of state governors veto it.

40. Maria is interested in politics and wants to run for office. What organization should she contact in order to become a candidate?
    A. a city council
    B. the state legislature
    C. a political party
    D. a corporation

41. The legislative branch of any level of government in the United States is responsible for which of the following?
    A. enacting laws to provide for public services
    B. enforcing laws against pollution
    C. sentencing people convicted of crimes
    D. appointing people to serve as judges

42. Which of the following documents established the three branches of the U.S. government?
    A. U.S. Constitution
    B. Bill of Rights
    C. Northwest Ordinance
    D. Declaration of Independence

43. In the map below, in which of the following coordinates is the state of Ohio located?
    A. V,9
    B. T,4
    C. Y,10
    D. X,5

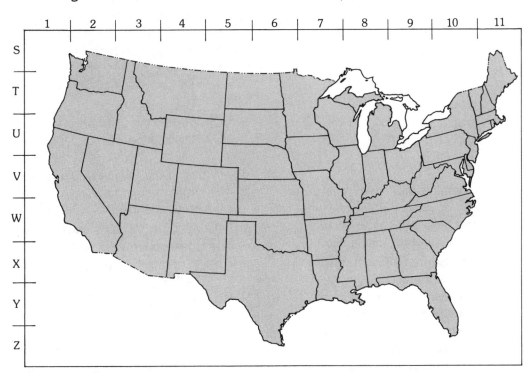

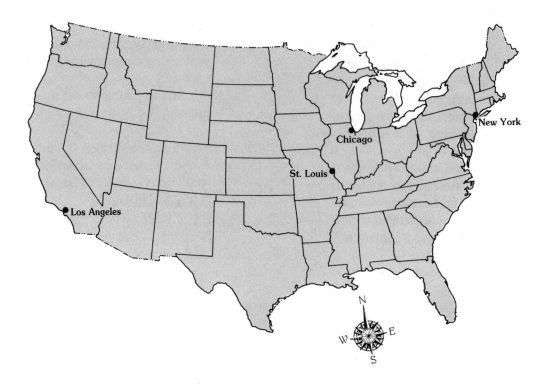

44. According to the map above, in which direction would you travel if you went from New York, New York, to Chicago, Illinois?
    A. north
    B. south
    C. west
    D. east

45. After identical bills have been passed by both houses of Congress, what is the next step that has to occur before the act becomes a law?
    A. The Supreme Court must review the act.
    B. The act must be sent to a conference committee.
    C. Both houses of Congress must debate the act.
    D. The president must sign the act.

46. The document that most clearly establishes for U.S. citizens such fundamental rights and freedoms as freedom of speech and the right to trial by jury is the
    A. Monroe Doctrine.
    B. Bill of Rights.
    C. Northwest Ordinance.
    D. Declaration of Independence.

47. Which of the following is **not** an example of economic interdependence?
    A. Country A raises corn and sells it to countries B and C.
    B. Country B mines iron ore and sells it to countries A and C.
    C. Country C manufactures automobiles and sells them to countries A and B.
    D. Country A grows wheat and sells it to bakeries in Country A.

48. Jack wants to write a letter to the editor of his local newspaper about the current election campaign for U.S. senator. But before he can write, he needs to check some of the facts that he has obtained about each candidate. From which of the following could he get the most accurate information?

  A. political advertisements on television
  B. each candidate's campaign manager
  C. newspaper articles about the campaign
  D. paid political advertisements in the newspapers

49. Adrienne wants a driver's license. From which level of government could she obtain a license?

  A. state
  B. city
  C. county
  D. national

50. Which two economic systems are most closely related to each other?

  A. capitalism and communism
  B. socialism and capitalism
  C. communism and socialism
  D. despotism and capitalism

GLOSSARY

absolute location   the exact location of a place, as indicated on a map by intersecting and numbered lines of latitude and longitude.

absolute monarchy   a form of government in which one person has unlimited power and, after the ruler's death, passes along that power to members of his or her family.

amendment   a formal change or addition to a bill, law, or constitution.

Anti-Federalists   those who opposed the ratification of the U.S. Constitution in 1787 and 1788.

Articles of Confederation   the document that provided the first plan of government for the United States in the 1780s.

bill   a formal proposal for a law.

Bill of Rights   the first ten amendments to the U.S. Constitution, which guarantee certain basic rights and freedoms to U.S. citizens.

Cabinet   a group of officials who act as advisors to the president and also as the heads of the various departments of the executive branch. Also, in state government, top advisors to the governor.

capital   a city where the lawmakers and chief executive of a nation or state have their offices.

capitalism   an economic system based on the profit motive, private ownership, competition, and the free market.

cardinal directions   the four main directions on a compass: north, south, east, and west.

checks and balances   a system for giving to each branch of government the ability to oppose the actions and policies of the other branches.

city council   a group of officials elected to make laws for a city.

city manager   an official appointed by the city council to direct the work of the city's executive departments.

civic activity   a voluntary act of community service.

civil servant   a government employee who is hired on the basis of that person's skills and training (not the person's politics).

commerce   trade, or the exchange of goods and services, on a large scale.

committee   a small group of legislators who study bills on a particular subject and recommend some of them to the other legislators.

communism   the economic theory that calls for goods and services to be equally distributed in some future society, which would have no social classes and no government.

compass rose   a map symbol used to show direction.

concurrent powers   those powers, such as collecting taxes and providing services, that belong to both the national and state government.

conference committee   a group of legislators selected from both houses of Congress or a state legislature. Its purpose is to agree on a single bill that will be acceptable to both houses.

Congress   the elected, lawmaking branch of the U.S. government.

"consent of the governed"   the idea that a nation's laws should have the approval of the people's elected representatives.

constitution   the basic plan for organizing and giving powers to a government.

constitutional monarchy   a form of government in which the powers of the monarch (ruler) are strictly limited by law.

Constitution of the United States   the document created in 1787 and ratified in 1788 that has served ever since as the basic plan of government and the "supreme law" of the United States.

council-manager system   a form of city government in which an elected city council appoints the city's chief executive—the city manager.

court of appeals   a court that may review the decisions of lower courts, or trial courts.

court of common pleas   one of many courts that conduct trials in the judicial branch of Ohio's government.

cross-examine   to question a witness at a trial after the witness has answered the questions of the opposing lawyer.

cultural diversity   a mixture of many distinct cultures.

Declaration of Independence   the document, written mainly by Thomas Jeffer-

son in 1776, that explains to the world why the United States demanded its independence from British rule.

delegated powers   those powers belonging to the federal government.

democracy   a form of government in which citizens elect their leaders and have the opportunity to make laws, either directly or indirectly.

democratic socialism   an economic and political system in which free elections are held and some major industries are under government ownership.

dictatorship   a form of government in which one person has total or nearly total control of the political system. Unlike a monarch, the dictator usually seizes power rather than inheriting it.

direct democracy   a form of government in which citizens meet in an assembly and make laws directly by majority vote.

directional arrow   a map symbol consisting of an arrow that points in one direction, north.

discrimination   unequal treatment of someone based on that person's physical or social traits.

district courts   those courts in the federal government that conduct trials.

double jeopardy   the practice (banned by the Fifth Amendment) by which a criminal suspect could be tried more than once for the same crime.

due process   fair procedures for arresting a criminal suspect and conducting a trial.

economics   the study of how people choose to use scarce resources to satisfy their needs and wants.

Eighth Amendment   the section of the U.S. Constitution that prohibits cruel and unusual punishments.

e pluribus unum   Latin phrase that means "one out of many."

equator   the imaginary line that runs east and west around the middle of the Earth.

equity   fair and equal application of the rights and protections guaranteed by the U.S. Constitution.

executive branch   the part of government whose chief function is to enforce, or carry out, the laws.

executive power   a government's power to enforce, or carry out, the laws.

exports   goods or services from one country that are sold to other countries.

Federalists   those who favored the ratification of the U.S. Constitution in 1787 and 1788.

federal system   (federalism) a type of government in which laws are made by both a national government and separate state governments.

Fifteenth Amendment   a section of the Constitution that, in effect, guarantees the right to vote to African Americans.

Fifth Amendment   a section of the Constitution that spells out the rights of accused persons, including the right to due process of law.

First Amendment   a section of the Constitution that guarantees freedom of religion, speech, press, assembly, and petition.

flowchart   a diagram showing the parts of a step-by-step procedure.

Fourth Amendment   a section of the Constitution that protects citizens from "unreasonable searches and seizures" of their property.

free market system   an economic system that permits privately owned businesses the freedom to decide what goods and services to offer for sale; another term for capitalism.

general election   an election (usually in early November) in which voters choose among candidates of different parties for particular government offices.

House of Representatives   the lower and larger house of Congress whose members represent districts of roughly equal population. Also the larger house of Ohio's General Assembly.

immigrant   a person who comes to a country to reside there permanently.

income tax   a tax on the income of an individual or a business.

incumbent   an elected person who currently occupies a government office.

Independence Day   July 4, the anniversary of the day in 1776 when Congress adopted the Declaration of Independence.

initiative   a procedure by which citizens can propose a law and place it on the ballot for the voters to accept or reject.

interdependence   a condition in which people or nations mutually depend upon one another.

interstate commerce   business activity or trade that is carried on in two or more states.

judicial branch   the part of government whose function is to conduct trials and interpret laws in specific cases.

judicial power   the power to interpret laws and conduct trials in a courtroom.

judicial review   the power of the U.S. Supreme Court and other courts to determine whether or not a law is allowed by the Constitution.

jury   a group of citizens chosen to hear evidence in a court case.

latitude, lines of imaginary lines on a map or globe that run east and west around the Earth.

legend a section of a map that explains the symbols used on the map.

legislative branch the part of government whose function is to make the laws.

legislative power a government's power to make laws.

limited monarchy a form of government headed by a monarch (ruler) whose authority is limited by law and custom.

literacy test a practice (no longer legal) by which potential voters could be disqualified from voting if examiners found that they could not read or write.

lobbyist someone employed by a special interest group to influence the votes of lawmakers.

longitude, lines of imaginary lines on a map or globe that run north and south between the North and South Poles.

Marxist socialism an economic system based on the theories of Karl Marx, a 19th-century German thinker. As practiced in the former Soviet Union and other countries, a single political party—the Communist party—controlled almost all aspects of a country's economic and political life.

mayor an elected official who serves as a city's chief executive.

means of production the machinery, tools, buildings, and lands that people use to produce wealth.

name-calling the effort to damage a political opponent by using a negative-sounding name to characterize him or her.

naturalization the process by which an immigrant can become a citizen.

Nineteenth Amendment a section of the U.S. Constitution that, in effect, guarantees women the right to vote.

nominate to select a political party's candidates for election.

Northwest Ordinance a document of 1787 that provided a plan of government for the Northwest Territory and guaranteed basic rights to settlers of that territory.

Northwest Territory the region north and west of the Ohio River that eventually became five states, including Ohio.

opportunity costs the possible uses of a resource that are given up when a person, government, or business decides how the resource shall actually be used.

organization chart a visual device for showing levels of power and responsibility in a government agency, business firm, or other large organization.

override to enact a bill into law after the chief executive (president or governor) has vetoed it.

platform a document stating a political party's positions on various issues.

"The Pledge of Allegiance" a formal oath of loyalty to the American flag and the nation for which it stands.

political party an organization whose members nominate candidates for government office and help their candidates win election.

polls places where citizens go to vote.

poll tax a fee that some states once required voters to pay before they could vote (now prohibited by the Twenty-fourth Amendment).

pressure group an organization that tries to influence laws that directly affect the organization and its members.

primary an election in which voters choose a political party's candidates for the coming general election.

probable cause a good reason for the police to believe that their search of someone's property is directly related to some criminal charge.

profit the money left over to a business after subtracting a business's total costs from its total sales.

projections a method of representing a three-dimensional area (Earth's surface) on a flat surface (map).

property tax a yearly tax on the value of buildings and land.

quota an upper limit on something, such as the number of immigrants permitted to come to the United States.

ratify to approve something, such as a constitutional amendment.

referendum a procedure that allows voters to directly approve or disapprove a proposed law.

relative location a way of identifying a place on a map by saying what places surround it.

repeal to remove an existing law.

representative democracy a form of government in which elected representatives of the people have the power to enact laws.

republic any form of government that permits the common people to elect government leaders and lawmakers.

reserved powers those powers belonging to the states that are allowed by the U.S. Constitution.

resource anything that has economic value.

sales tax a tax based upon the selling price of various items.

scale of distance a device for measuring distances between points on a map.

scarcity the idea that economic resources are never enough to satisfy everybody's needs.

search warrant a legal document issued by a judge that allows police officers to search specified buildings, property, or persons.

secretary a high government official who assists the chief executive.

self-incrimination a confession or other statement by a person that would make that person appear to be guilty of a crime.

Senate the upper and smaller house of Congress or a state legislature.

separation of powers the principle of dividing three types of power (legislative, executive, and judicial) among three separate branches of government.

share of stock a share of ownership in a business.

Sixth Amendment a section of the U.S. Constitution that guarantees certain rights to a person standing trial for a crime.

socialism an economic system in which major industries are publicly owned and controlled by the government.

Social Security tax a federal tax collected from workers' wages in order to support older persons who have retired from the work force as well as widows and their dependent children.

"The Star-Spangled Banner" the national anthem, or official song, of the

United States. Words to the song were written by Francis Scott Key during the War of 1812.

suffrage   the right to vote.

Supreme Court   the highest (most powerful) court in the U.S. court system and state court system.

taxation   a government's practice of collecting money from citizens in order to finance public services.

third party   any U.S. political party that is smaller than either of the two major parties (Democratic and Republican).

titles of nobility   an official name or rank that carries with it special honors and privileges. Often the title is one that can be inherited by the person's heirs. Such titles for U.S. citizens are prohibited by the U.S. Constitution.

unconstitutional   contrary to the U.S. Constitution or a state constitution.

verify   to prove correct.

veto   the power of a president or governor to stop a bill from becoming law by refusing to sign it.

Western Hemisphere   the half of the Earth that includes North and South America and surrounding waters.

zoning laws   local laws that divide a community into regions, or zones, according to their use.

INDEX